# How to Deep-fat Fry

1. Coat meat with seasoned flour or corn meal, egg and crumbs, or batter.
2. Fry a few servings at a time in enough lard to cover the meat, using approximately 350° F. temperature for frying.
3. Continue cooking until meat is done inside and is golden brown and crisp outside.
4. Remove from frying kettle and drain; serve at once.

# How to Braise

1. Brown meat on all sides in hot fat in heavy utensil.
2. Season with salt and pepper.
3. Add small amount of liquid, if necessary.
4. Cover tightly.
5. Cook at simmering temperature until tender.

# How to Simmer (LARGE CUTS)

1. Cover meat with hot or cold water.
2. Season with salt and pepper. Cover kettle tightly.
3. Cook slowly. Allow to simmer, not boil.
4. Add vegetables, if desired, just long enough before serving to be cooked.

# How to Simmer (STEWS)

1. Cut meat in 1 to 2 inch cubes.
2. Brown on all sides in hot lard, if desired.
3. Season with salt and pepper.
4. Cover with water and cover kettle tightly.
5. Cook slowly until done.
6. Add vegetables just long enough before serving to be cooked.

# The Lamb Cookbook

# The Lamb Cookbook

## BY PAULA OWEN

RANDOM HOUSE  NEW YORK

# TABLE OF CONTENTS

# INTRODUCTORY NOTE

At best, today's life is fast-paced and hectic for most of us. The role of the homemaker is, therefore, more important than ever, because it becomes her duty to make her home a haven from the cares of the world . . . a place where family members may become refreshed in body and spirit.

The serving of tasty, well-balanced meals is important to the family's well-being, but just as important as the food itself is the atmosphere in which a meal is served. Dinnertime should be a time for family reunion after the work of the day . . . a time to relax and enjoy good food and good conversation. Mealtime is not the time for airing knotty problems or quarrels, nor is it a time for gulping a hastily prepared meal from a tray in front of the television set.

It is the author's hope that the following lamb recipes and suggestions will serve as an inspiration to serve tasty, well-balanced meals. Your family will benefit.

Lamb is, first of all, an excellent source of high-quality protein. Since in most cuts the fat is easily separable from the lean, calories can be held down where this is desirable. Lamb is a good source of phosphorus, magnesium and iron, thiamine, riboflavin and niacin. Lamb is also easily digested, making these food elements readily available for the body's use rather quickly. Thus lamb becomes what we might call a "quick energy" meat, ideal for the diets of all age groups.

# The Lamb Cookbook

# ALL ABOUT LAMB

## Availability of Lamb

More lambs are born in the spring and summer months than in the rest of the year. This means that more lambs are available for consumption in the fall. This is also likely to be the time of year when prices are lowest. While lamb used to be considered seasonal meat, this is no longer the case. A supply is now available the year 'round, even though there are still some periods of the year when the supply is more abundant than in others.

## Lamb Marketing

All reputable retailers and packers selling "lamb" as such, are selling meat *less than a year old* regardless of the carcass weight; and the grade, whether packer brand or government grade, will denote its quality. Because of improved breeding and feeding, many lambs (less than a year old) are coming to market weighing over 60 pounds dressed. These are not necessarily overly fat, but are a meatier variety that represents an excellent value.

In broad terms, lambs from three to five months of age are often called "Genuine Spring Lambs." This is a misleading term, however, inasmuch as lambs in this category are available at widely varying times of the year, depending upon where they were raised—in the East, North, South, or West. Climatic conditions are responsible for the varying production season. A better term, growing in its usage, is "Milk Finished Lambs." The carcasses of Milk Finished Lambs will average 30 to 45 pounds. In many areas, lambs just a bit older, those falling in the six- to twelve-month age bracket, are called "Springers." This, too, is a misleading term. A better one is "Fed Finished Lambs." Fed Finished Lambs will run about 45 to 60 pounds dressed, as a rule.

Sometimes in January, February and March, one sees "Hot House" or "Baby" lambs on the market in some areas. These normally range from six to eight weeks in age and weigh approximately 17 to 25 pounds. "Yearlings" are one year old, but less than two. They will average a year and a half in age, and 55 to 70 pounds in weight. "Mutton" is usually one and a half to two years of age when slaughtered, or it may be older. Ninety-four per cent of all ovines slaughtered in this country, however, are lambs. *All* grades are found in weight categories from 30 to 60 pounds. The above categories and terms must be considered only as broad general classifications.

### Differentiation of Lamb, Yearling and Mutton Carcasses

Lamb, yearling and mutton carcasses are classified according to the differences that occur in the development of their muscular and skeletal systems.

Lamb carcasses have break joints in their fore shanks and narrow rib bones. The meat is fine-textured. Their forequarters are usually narrow and compact. When the forefeet of young lambs are broken off at the break joint, a series of well-defined points will be exposed (usually eight). With advancing age these become rounded and decrease in number. Yearling mutton carcasses may have either break joints or "spool" joints. The rib bones will be a bit wider. The lean meat will be slightly coarser in texture and slightly darker red in color. Mutton carcasses always have "spool" joints on their front shanks, and usually have wide rib bones and a wide "spready" forequarter. The break joint cannot be broken in mutton, so this joint provides the simplest way to distinguish lamb from mutton.

High quality lamb has a smooth covering of clear, pinkish-white, brittle fat over most of the exterior. Over this is a thin, paperlike covering called the "fell." It is usually removed from chops before cooking. Under normal conditions, it should *not* be removed from the legs as this cut will hold its shape better, be more juicy and cook faster when the fell is left on.

Most cuts of lamb are tender since the meat comes from young animals, so they are usually cooked by dry heat. Legs, loins, shoulders and racks may be roasted; steaks and loin, rib and shoulder *chops* may be broiled, panbroiled or griddle-broiled. Shoulder chops are often exceptionally good braised. All cuts of lamb, regardless of cookery method used, should be cooked at low temperatures for best results. There are just three rules for cooking lamb. (1) Cook according to cut. (2) Always use low temperatures. (3) Avoid overcooking.

### Fresh Lamb

When fresh lamb is brought home from the market, it should be stored in the coldest part of the refrigerator. Many wrappings today are specially treated to preserve the "bloom" or attractiveness of the meat, and need not be removed. If in doubt, however, unwrap and cover loosely with waxed paper.

The temperature for storing uncooked lamb should range between 32 degrees and 40 degrees F. Higher temperatures affect the keeping qualities while lower temperatures will freeze the meat.

Ground lamb should be kept in the coldest spot, since it does not have the keeping qualities of lamb which has not been ground. When it is necessary to hold ground lamb more than 24 hours, it may be carefully wrapped in freezer paper to exclude all air, and then frozen.

Variety meats, such as liver, kidney and heart, do not keep as well as muscle meats. Use them as soon after purchasing as possible; or if they are to be held, they should be frozen or precooked.

### Frozen Lamb

A temperature of zero degrees F. or lower should be maintained in storing frozen lamb. It may be defrosted during cooking, at room temperature, or in the refrigerator if time permits. Frozen lamb which has been defrosted should be cooked as soon as it is defrosted. Do not refreeze.

### Cooked Lamb

Lamb which has been cooked should be stored in the refrigerator, covered, to prevent drying. When the amount of cooked lamb is small it is desirable to remove the bone before storing, to save space and prevent drying.

Left-over cooked lamb broth, stock, soup, sauces and gravies should be covered and placed in the refrigerator as soon as the meal is over.

### Basic Cookery Methods

There are three basic cookery methods to use in preparing lamb as in cooking other meats. (1) *Dry heat.* This method includes roasting, broiling and panbroiling. (2) *Moist heat.* Moist heat cookery includes braising and cooking in liquid (such as stews). (3) *Frying.* Lamb may be panfried or griddle-fried, and in some cases, as in making ground lamb fritters, deep-fat fried.

### Temperatures in Roasting

For roasting, a low temperature of 300 degrees F. is recommended. Low temperatures help a roast to become more uniformly done throughout. Shrinkage and flow of juices will be moderate. The roast will be more attractive to serve and will in most instances have a better flavor. High roasting temperatures, when used throughout the roasting period or for most of it, cause waste through excessive shrinkage. The meat will be less juicy and unevenly cooked, and charring of bones is likely. Moisture losses which occur in roasting are of two kinds—evaporation and dripping loss. It is highly desirable to keep down these losses. If the oven has no regulator, an oven thermometer is recommended. Tests conducted by the home economics department of a well-known packing company provide the following interesting information obtained by roasting three frozen, boned, rolled shoulders of lamb, all to an internal temperature of 160 degrees.

300 degrees F.—Shrank 26.5%—took 46 minutes to the pound
325 degrees F.—Shrank 31.2%—took 42 minutes to the pound
350 degrees F.—Shrank 37.5%—took 36 minutes to the pound

The interesting thing is that the higher the roasting temperature, the greater the losses.

### Searing

Searing of a lamb roast is not recommended. The old theory that searing holds in meat juices and decreases cooking losses has been disproved.

### Basting

Basting is desirable only when roasting on a revolving spit, barbecue fashion, or when a glaze or flavor-adding sauce is used. It is not necessary when oven-roasting a plain roast. For self-basting, place roast in pan, fat side up. As the meat cooks, the melting fat will run over and into the meat sufficiently. If too much fat is present pour off drippings. A rack is recommended to hold roast up out of the drippings.

### To Cover or Not to Cover the Roaster?

A lamb roast should be cooked uncovered. In a covered pan, the end product is not a roast, because it will in reality be cooked in moisture, since the moisture which escapes from the meat is held inside the roaster. The meat will be tasty, but not a true roast.

Serving Temperature

Lamb is best served piping hot on hot plates, or sliced, chilled. Lukewarm lamb lacks the full flavor found in the piping hot or chilled meat.

When to Salt

This point seems to cause much concern. To sum up the situation briefly, most experts agree that in the case of roasts, stews and braised meats, it makes little difference when the salt is added. In roasting, salt penetrates only to a depth of about an inch. Since salt is said to draw juices up out of the meat, in the case of chops and steaks where a large open cut surface is exposed, as in broiling, it is felt by most authorities that it is wisest to brown the chop or steak, salt, turn, brown and salt the second side before removing from broiler.

Tongs or Fork for Turning?

In turning lamb chops and steaks, tongs are felt to be a little better than a fork which pricks the meat, allowing juices to escape. If a fork must be used for turning meat, try to insert it in the fat around the edge of the chop or steak for maximum juice retention.

The Popliteal and Prescapular Glands in Lamb

The popliteal gland occurs just above the hock joint in a leg of lamb. This gland, sometimes referred to as the "musk gland," is mistakenly believed by some to cause an odor in cooking and sometimes a strong flavor. A similar gland, the prescapular, is found in the shoulder, and is seldom or never removed. Both these glands are in reality lymph glands. They are approximately as large in the small animal as in the more mature ones and are, therefore, by comparison, more conspicuous in the small animals. These glands should cause the consumer no concern whatever, inasmuch as many cooking and taste tests have been conducted by various groups, and such tests have proved conclusively that the glands have absolutely no effect on either odor or flavor of lamb. The identical glands are found in beef and pork also and are removed only if the surrounding fat makes a cut look undesirable. The only thing that can cause an undesirable odor in cooking lamb is using too high a cooking temperature. Burning fat is unpleasant to the sense of smell no matter what kind of meat one is cooking. Hold roasting temperatures to 300 degrees F. for best results all around.

### Is It Safe to Serve Lamb Underdone?

Perfectly safe. While the popular preference is largely for medium to well-done lamb there is no reason why lamb cannot be served at any degree of doneness desired. Lambs are clean and unusually healthy. They are not subject to trichinosis so there is no reason why the meat has to be served well done. More and more people are learning to like lamb cooked to an internal temperature of 170 degrees F. or less. When the meat is still slightly pink, it is unusually juicy and flavorful.

### After Removal from Oven

The internal temperatures of *large* roasts will rise after they are removed from the oven, and the meat will continue to cook a little for some time. This should be kept in mind in the event the cook has developed a taste for underdone meat. A "rest" period of from 15 to 20 minutes is desirable after the roast is removed from the oven, as this gives the meat a chance to "firm up" and makes slicing easier. The roast should, of course, be placed in a warm place for this firming-up process.

### Preparing the Less Expensive Lamb Cuts

Lamb's goodness is due in large part to its tenderness and to the flavor imparted by its fat. In some of the thriftier cuts, however, it is desirable to dispose of excess fat before and during cooking. In the case of riblets, for example, which are so wonderful barbecued, it is suggested that excess fat be trimmed away before cooking and that after browning, the drippings be poured off before sauce is added. Remembering to do this will make such inexpensive dishes so popular with families that the homemaker can save money on her budget often. Don't be afraid of fatter cuts. Just dispose of the fat, and the resulting fare will be more than worth the effort required.

# TIMETABLE FOR COOKING LAMB

*Lamb is very easy to cook and may be prepared by any of the basic cookery methods used in preparing other red meats. As a guide, and for handy general reference, however, the following table may be useful.*

| CUT | Roasted at 300° F. Oven Temperature | | Broiled[1] | Braised | Simmered |
| | Meat Thermometer Reading | Time Minutes per Pound | (Minutes) Total Time | (Hours) Total Time | (Hours) Total Time |
| --- | --- | --- | --- | --- | --- |
| LEG | 175-180° | 30 to 35 | | | |
| SHOULDER | | | | | |
| Whole | 175-180° | 30 to 35 | | | |
| Rolled | 175-180° | 40 to 45 | | | |
| Cushion | 175-180° | 30 to 35 | | | |
| BREAST | | | | | |
| Stuffed | 175-180° | 30 to 35 | | 1½-2 | |
| Rolled | 175-180° | 30 to 35 | | 1½-2 | |
| LAMB LOAF | 175-180° | 30 to 35 | | | |
| CHOPS (1 inch) | | | 12 | | |
| CHOPS (1½ inch) | | | 18 | | |
| CHOPS (2 inch) | | | 22 | | |
| LAMB PATTIES (1 inch) | | | 15-18 | | |
| NECK SLICES | | | | 1 | |
| SHANKS | | | | 1½ | |
| STEW | | | | | 1½-2 |
| LIVER | | | 8-10 | | |
| KIDNEYS | | | 10-12 | | |
| HEART | | | | 2½-3 | 2½-3 |
| SWEETBREADS[2] | | | 10-15 | 20-25* | 15-20* |
| BRAINS | | | 10-15 | 20-25* | 15-20* |

* Minutes.

[1] Panbroiling or griddle-broiling requires approximately one-half as much time as broiling.

[2] Times for sweetbreads are those required after they have been precooked in water and membrane removed.

# LAMB

*Based on Research of R. M. Leverton, Ph.D., 1958*
*Nutrient Content of Cooked Meats 100 GM.*

| Lamb Cut | Cooked Weight Oz. | Measured as Consumed | Protein Gm. | Calories | Calcium mg. |
|---|---|---|---|---|---|
| Arm Chop | 3½ | | 25.7 | 252 | |
| Blade Chop | 3½ | 4" x 2" x ¾th | 27.4 | 280 | |
| Loin Chop | 3½ | | 27.1 | 223 | 8.2 |
| Rib Chop | 3½ | | 25.5 | 291 | |
| Roast Leg, Whole | 3½ | 4" x 3" x ½th | 28.2 | 195 | 8.2 |
| Roast Leg, Center Cut | 3½ | | 28.3 | 182 | |
| Riblets | 3½ | | 23.5 | 399 | |

\* Calculated Dr. Schweigert's Bulletin #30. Blank spaces indicate no analysis made.

| Phosphorus Mg. | Magnesium Mg. | Iron* Mg. | Thiamine Mg. | Riboflavin Mg. | Niacin Mg. |
|---|---|---|---|---|---|
| 236 | 24.5 | | | | |
| 243 | 23.4 | | | | |
| 214 | 24.1 | 2.8 | 0.21 | 0.33 | 7.9 |
| 220 | 20.4 | 2.8 | | | |
| 215 | 23.6 | 3.6 | 0.23 | 0.31 | 7.3 |
| | 23.3 | | | | |
| 158 | 19.5 | | | | |

# Lamb Cuts

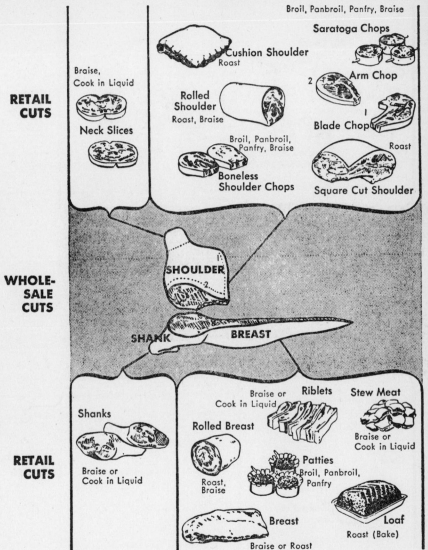

**RETAIL CUTS**

Broil, Panbroil, Panfry, Braise

Saratoga Chops

Cushion Shoulder
Roast

Arm Chop
2

Braise,
Cook in Liquid

Rolled
Shoulder
Roast, Braise

Blade Chop
1

Neck Slices

Broil, Panbroil,
Panfry, Braise

Roast

Boneless
Shoulder Chops

Square Cut Shoulder

**WHOLE-SALE CUTS**

SHOULDER
1
2

SHANK          BREAST

**RETAIL CUTS**

Braise or          Riblets          Stew Meat
Cook in Liquid

Shanks

Rolled Breast

Braise or
Cook in Liquid

Patties
Broil, Panbroil,
Panfry

Braise or
Cook in Liquid

Roast,
Braise

Breast          Loaf

Roast (Bake)

Braise or Roast

# and How to Cook Them

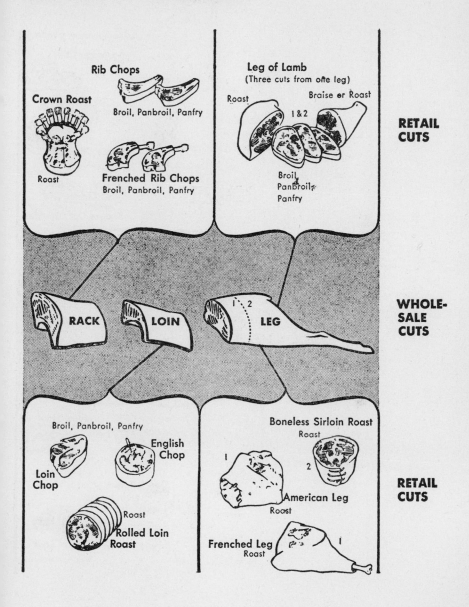

**Rib Chops**
Broil, Panbroil, Panfry

**Crown Roast**
Roast

**Frenched Rib Chops**
Broil, Panbroil, Panfry

**Leg of Lamb**
(Three cuts from one leg)
Roast
Braise or Roast
1 & 2
Broil
Panbroil
Panfry

**RETAIL CUTS**

RACK    LOIN    LEG    1  2

**WHOLE-SALE CUTS**

Broil, Panbroil, Panfry
**Loin Chop**
**English Chop**
Roast
**Rolled Loin Roast**

**Boneless Sirloin Roast**
Roast
1
2
**American Leg**
Roast
**Frenched Leg**
Roast
1

**RETAIL CUTS**

# HOW TO
# CARVE LAMB

First, see to it that the knife is very sharp before carving is started.

Place the leg of lamb before the carver so that the thick meaty section is on the far side of the platter. The illustrations show a right leg being carved. With the left leg, the shank bone is at the opposite end, or to carver's left, but this does not affect the method of carving.

Insert the fork firmly in the large end and carve two or three lengthwise slices from the near thin side (top illustration).

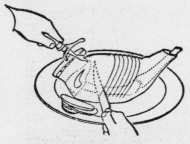

Turn the roast so it rests on surface just cut. The shank bone now points up from the platter.

Insert the fork in the left end of the roast. Starting at the shank end, slice down to the leg bone. Make parallel slices until aitch bone is reached (center illustration). One-fourth to three-eighths inch is desirable thickness.

With the fork still in place, run the knife along the leg bone, releasing all slices (bottom illustration).

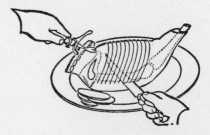

# PART 1

## Lamb Is Basic

# APPETIZERS

*Hot hors d'oeuvres are extra good made from lamb.
Try these new ideas. Since many hostesses enjoy
serving a variety of hot hors d'oeuvres, two recipes
for curries appropriate for this purpose are
included in this section. These are best served
from small plates with forks, at parties where
guests can be seated.*

▪▪▪▪▪▪▪▪▪▪▪▪▪▪▪▪▪▪▪▪▪▪▪▪▪▪▪▪▪▪▪▪▪▪▪▪▪▪▪▪▪▪

## TINY LAMB KEBABS

(Makes about 3 dozen)

1 pound boneless lamb
  shoulder
1 3½-ounce jar cocktail
  onions

1 6-ounce can tomato paste
1 tablespoon sugar
½ teaspoon salt
¼ teaspoon pepper

Cut lamb into ½-inch cubes. Drain onions, reserving liquid.
Arrange lamb and onions on toothpicks. Broil 3 to 4 inches
from source of heat 4 or 5 minutes, or until lightly browned.
Combine onion liquid and remaining ingredients. Heat to
serving temperature, stirring occasionally. Serve tomato
mixture as a dip for lamb kebabs.

## GRILLED LAMB APPETIZER KEBABS

(4 servings)

2 cups 1½-inch cubes cooked     1 cup cooked small white
    lamb                                          onions
1 medium-sized tomato, diced    4 strips bacon

Arrange lamb, tomato and onions on skewers. Wrap with
bacon. Broil 3 to 4 inches from source of heat 5 to 7 minutes, or until bacon is crisp on all sides.

## LAMB CAVIAR CANAPÉ

(Makes about 3 cups)

2 tablespoons salad oil          2 tablespoons black caviar
1 pound ground lamb              Salt and pepper to taste
1 cup chopped eggplant

Heat oil; add lamb and eggplant and cook over low heat
until browned, stirring occasionally. Add remaining ingredients; mix well. Serve as a spread for crackers, as desired.

## LITTLE LAMBIE TARTS

(Makes about 24 1¾-inch tarts)

2 tablespoons butter or          1 teaspoon salt
    margarine                        Dash cayenne pepper
1 pound ground lamb              Dash Tabasco sauce
¼ pound mushrooms,               1 cup sifted all-purpose flour
    chopped                          ½ teaspoon salt
1 tablespoon Worcestershire      ⅓ cup shortening
    sauce                            ¼ cup milk

Melt butter or margarine. Add lamb, mushrooms, Worcester-shire sauce, 1 teaspoon salt, cayenne pepper and Tabasco sauce. Cook over low heat 20 minutes, or until browned, stirring occasionally. Meanwhile, combine flour and ½ tea-spoon salt. Cut in shortening with pastry blender or two knives. Add milk and mix lightly. Press into ball. Roll out on lightly floured surface to ⅛-inch thickness. Cut in rounds. Press into 1¾-inch muffin pans. Prick bottoms. Bake in hot oven (400°) 10 minutes, or until lightly browned. Serve filled with lamb mixture.

## FESTIVE LAMB TARTS

(Makes 10 tarts)

1 cup sifted all-purpose flour
½ teaspoon salt
⅓ cup shortening
2-3 tablespoons water
½ pound ground lamb
3 tablespoons mayonnaise
3 tablespoons softened
    cream cheese
½ cup grated processed
    American cheese
Dash Tabasco sauce
2 tablespoons grated onion
½ teaspoon curry powder
¼ cup finely chopped
    pimiento-stuffed green
    olives
Parsley

Combine flour and salt. Cut in shortening. Add water and mix lightly. Press into ball. Roll out on lightly floured sur-face to ⅛-inch thickness. Cut into ten 2¾-inch circles, using floured cutter. Press into 2½-inch tart pans and prick. Bake in hot oven (450°) 10 to 12 minutes or until lightly browned. Cool. Meanwhile, cook lamb over low heat 15 minutes, or until thoroughly cooked. Drain off drippings. Blend mayon-naise, cheeses, Tabasco sauce, onion, curry powder and olives. Fold in lamb. Fill tarts with lamb mixture and gar-nish with parsley.

## MINIATURE LAMB PIZZAS

(Makes about 30 2-inch pizzas)

4 cups biscuit mix
1 cup milk
1 8-ounce can tomato sauce
1 pound ground lamb
½ pound Mozzarella cheese, sliced

¼ cup grated Parmesan cheese
2 teaspoons oregano
1 teaspoon salt

Combine biscuit mix and milk; mix lightly. Turn out on lightly floured surface. Knead gently ten times. Roll out to ¼-inch thickness. Cut into rounds with floured 2-inch cutter. Place on baking sheets. Top with tomato sauce, lamb and Mozzarella cheese. Sprinkle with remaining ingredients. Bake in hot oven (425°) 15 to 20 minutes, or until lightly browned.

## LAMB TOAST APPETIZERS

(Makes 3½ dozen)

1 1-pound loaf white sliced bread (14 slices)
¼ cup melted butter or margarine
2 tablespoons celery seeds
¼ cup mayonnaise
1 small onion, finely chopped

¼ teaspoon paprika
2 teaspoons chopped parsley
1 tablespoon prepared horse-radish
1 teaspoon prepared mustard
1 teaspoon lemon juice
½ pound cooked ground lamb

Trim crusts from bread. Cut each slice into 3½x1-inch strips. Brush one side with butter or margarine and sprinkle with celery seeds. Place on baking sheet. Bake in hot oven (425°) 8 to 10 minutes on both sides, or until lightly browned. Blend remaining ingredients and spread on toast sticks. If desired, garnish sticks with sprigs of parsley or pimiento strips.

## LAMB CURRY

Boiled lamb shoulder, or
left-over roast of lamb
cut in ¾-inch cubes
⅓ cup seedless raisins

½ cup water or lamb stock
1 can condensed cream of
chicken soup
½-1 teaspoon curry powder

Simmer raisins in water or lamb stock about 5 minutes to plump them. Stir in the condensed cream of chicken soup and curry powder. Add lamb cubes and heat thoroughly. Serve hot over steamed rice. (Makes 1¾ cups sauce for similar amount of lamb.)

## LAMB ANTIPASTO

(6 servings)

¾ cup olive oil
¾ cup vinegar
1½ teaspoons oregano
1 clove garlic, chopped
12 slices cooked leg or
shoulder of lamb
½ pound mushrooms
Italian peppers
Italian tomatoes

Canned artichoke hearts
Onion rings
Canned rolled anchovy
fillets
Celery hearts
1 loaf Italian bread, sliced
½ pound Mozzarella cheese,
sliced
Paprika

Combine oil, vinegar, oregano and garlic; blend. Add lamb and mushrooms. Cover and chill 4 hours. Drain lamb and

and stock. Stir constantly, cooking until smooth and of a creamy consistency. Add orange peel and pour over cooked hot lamb meat balls. This sauce may be made in advance, refrigerated and heated just before serving.

## OVEN-BARBECUED LAMB RIBLETS

Lamb riblets (at least 2 to a person)

Thin barbecue sauce of some sort

Honey, warmed, for brushing on riblets

Powdered thyme

Place riblets close together in your favorite French dressing or in a thin barbecue sauce to cover; allow to stand in the sauce in the refrigerator several hours or overnight. To cook: Place on broiler pan about 2 to 3 inches below heat source in broiler oven. Cook one side of riblets to desired doneness, about 5 minutes. Turn, brush with dressing or sauce, cook about 4 minutes more. Remove from oven, brush tops liberally with warmed honey, sprinkle very lightly with powdered thyme. Slip pan back under broiler for the riblets to finish browning and to glaze. At the end of the broiling time (10 to 12 minutes), the riblets should be well browned and crispy-sided. Serve very hot.

*Note:* For easy handling, a bit of meat may be trimmed from rib ends. They may also be served with paper frills.

## BUTTER-BROWNED LAMB MARBLES

(Makes about 20)

1 pound lean ground lamb

½ teaspoon salt

Dash of pepper

¼ teaspoon onion salt

⅛ teaspoon garlic salt

⅛ teaspoon powdered thyme, if desired

½ teaspoon cornstarch

Mix all together lightly. Using a teaspoon for a measure, round up enough of the lamb on the spoon to make a ball about the size of a large marble. Roll in hands dipped in cold water. Place on shallow pan. Cover with wax paper and put in refrigerator until ready to use. The cornstarch helps hold the shape during cooking. To cook: Put 2 table-spoons butter in a shallow frying pan; heat to bubbly stage. Add the lamb and, as the balls start to brown, shake the pan to keep them rolling in the butter and browning on all sides. They need little cooking, consequently much watching. Stick a colorful cocktail pick through each little lamb marble. Serve from a casserole or other dish kept hot over a warmer of some sort.

### Lamb Marbles in Mushroom Caps

Prepare Lamb Marbles by browning in butter, as above. Place each marble in a medium-sized mushroom cap which has been heated and lightly browned in butter. Stick a colorful pick into the marble so that it will also go through the mushroom. Serve very hot, with or without Parmesan bread rounds.

## Dippin' Dunks

*for*
*Tiny Grilled or Broiled Lamb Nuggets on Picks or Cooked Bite-Sized Marbles of Ground Lamb*

1. Try mayonnaise to which prepared mustard has been added, or minced onion, dill pickle, and a bit of lemon juice. Or, mayonnaise with curry powder to suit your taste.

2. Puréed apple sauce with a bit of horse-radish stirred in. Or, try hot cinnamon-apple sauce, made by heating a No.

2 can of purée style apple sauce with ½ cup red cinnamon
candies until dissolved. Stir in a drop or two of extra
coloring, if needed. Keep hot over candle or on electric
trivet.

## 3. CHIVE DIP                    (Makes about 1¼ cups dip)

1 8-ounce package cream
    cheese, softened
¼ cup milk
2 tablespoons chopped
    chives

1 teaspoon garlic salt
1 teaspoon paprika
½ teaspoon salt

Combine cheese, milk, chives, garlic salt, paprika and
salt; blend. Chill cheese mixture and lamb. Place lamb
on cocktail picks before serving with chilled cheese mixture.

## 4. SOUR CREAM DIP          (Makes about 1½ cups dip)

1 cup commercial sour
    cream

½ cup grated carrot
1 tablespoon grated onion

Combine cream, carrots and onion; mix well. Chill before
serving with chilled lamb.

## 5. BARBECUE SAUCE DIP

⅓ cup water
¾ cup vinegar
⅓ cup butter
⅓ cup chili sauce
3 tablespoons grated
    horse-radish sauce

3 tablespoons Worcestershire
    sauce
½ teaspoon salt
Dash of cayenne pepper

Mix ingredients in saucepan. Simmer over low heat until
smooth and well blended—takes only a minute or so.
Two teaspoons sugar may be added to above if desired.

# SOUPS

*Everyone is familiar with the goodness of "Scotch broth" or "Scotch soup" made with lamb and barley as the two most basic ingredients. Don't be afraid to use lamb and lamb bones in making soup stock for various kinds of soups, however. You'll find it gives a unique flavor that is wonderful as a base for vegetable soup, or even for rice and tomato or split pea soup. In the following section you'll find many new ideas for lamb soups everyone will like.*

▀▄▀▄▀▄▀▄▀▄▀▄▀▄▀▄▀▄▀▄▀▄▀▄▀▄▀▄▀▄▀▄▀▄▀▄▀▄

## LAMB AND BARLEY SOUP

(8 servings)

| | |
|---|---|
| 2 tablespoons butter or margarine | 2 bay leaves |
| 1½ pounds ground lamb | ½ cup barley |
| 1 cup chopped onion | 1½ quarts water |
| 1 cup chopped celery | ¼ cup lemon juice |
| 1 cup sliced carrots | 1½ teaspoons salt |
| 1½ cups peas | ¼ teaspoon pepper |
| | ¼ cup chopped parsley |

Melt butter or margarine; add lamb, onions and celery. Cook until lamb is lightly browned, stirring occasionally.

Pour off excess fat, if any. Add carrots, peas, bay leaves, barley, water, lemon juice, salt and pepper. Cover and cook over low heat 45 minutes, or until vegetables are tender, stirring occasionally. Add parsley and mix well.

## LAMB BARLEY SOUP

(8 servings)

4 lamb neck slices (about 1½ pounds)
2 tablespoons shortening
1½ quarts water
2 teaspoons or more salt
Pepper
1 bay leaf
¼ cup barley
1 cup coarsely cut celery
1 cup sliced onions
1 cup sliced or diced carrots
¼ cup minced parsley
1 teaspoon sugar
1 clove garlic, mashed or minced
2 cups canned tomatoes

Brown lamb in shortening in heavy kettle or Dutch oven. Pour off excess fat, if any. Add water and remaining ingredients. Bring to boil, reduce heat, and simmer about 2½ hours. For added flavor, other vegetables, such as peas, mushrooms, string beans and green lima beans, may be added during the last half hour of cooking.

## SCOTCH SOUP

(4 to 6 servings)

1½ pounds lamb neck
1 quart cold water
2 medium onions, sliced
2 tablespoons barley or rice
2 potatoes, sliced
Salt to taste

Cut lamb from bones; place with bones in kettle with water. Cover. Cook slowly several hours. One hour before serving, remove bones, skim off fat, if necessary, and add remaining ingredients. Thicken with a little flour, if desired. The above can become a tasty lamb vegetable soup by the addition of carrots, tomatoes, green beans, etc.

## GOLDEN SOUP

(4 to 6 servings)

½ cup dried yellow peas
1 quart lamb stock
8 1-inch dry bread cubes
1 egg, beaten

2 tablespoons milk
Salt and pepper to taste
1 tablespoon chopped
    parsley

Cover dried peas with water and soak for 3 to 4 hours. Drain. Simmer peas in lamb stock until tender. Dip bread cubes in mixture of egg and milk; drop in soup. Cover. Simmer about 5 minutes. Season. Sprinkle with parsley.

## LAMB STOCK FOR GOLDEN SOUP

3 pounds lamb neck
3 quarts cold water
1 tablespoon salt
⅓ cup chopped celery
⅓ cup diced carrots

⅓ cup chopped onion
¼ cup chopped parsley
5 whole cloves
1 bay leaf

Cut meat from bones; brown well. Add remaining ingredients, cover, and simmer 3½ to 4 hours. Strain, chill, remove fat, strain again.

## LAMB AND CABBAGE SOUP

### (4 to 6 servings)

2 tablespoons salad oil
4 lamb shanks (about 4
    pounds)
1 large onion, sliced
1 medium-sized green
    pepper, diced

1 quart lamb stock or
    bouillon
1 teaspoon celery salt
1 teaspoon salt
¼ teaspoon pepper
1 small head of cabbage,
    coarsely shredded

Heat oil; add lamb and cook until lightly browned on all sides. Add onion, green pepper, stock or bouillon and seasonings. Cover and cook over low heat 1 hour, or until lamb is tender. Add cabbage. Cover and cook 15 minutes.

## LAMB CORN CHOWDER

### (6 to 8 servings)

2 tablespoons butter or
    margarine
1 pound ground lamb
4 medium-sized onions,
    chopped
4 medium-sized potatoes,
    diced

1 tablespoon salt
⅛ teaspoon pepper
3 cups water
1 quart milk
1 12-ounce can whole
    kernel corn

Melt butter or margarine. Add lamb and onions and cook until lightly browned. Pour off excess fat, if any. Add potatoes, salt, pepper and water. Cook covered over low heat about 15 minutes, or until potatoes are tender. Add milk and corn; mix well. Heat to serving temperature.

## LAMB CURRY TOMATO SOUP

(6 servings)

2 tablespoons butter or         2 1-pound cans tomatoes
  margarine                     2 cups water
1 pound ground lamb            1½ teaspoons curry powder
1 cup chopped celery            Salt and pepper to taste
1 cup chopped onion

Melt butter or margarine. Add lamb; cook until lightly browned. Pour off excess fat, if any. Add celery, onions, tomatoes, water and curry powder. Cover and cook over low heat 30 minutes. Season with salt and pepper.

## CHILI CON CARNE

(6 to 8 servings)

2 tablespoons fat or oil        1 clove garlic, mashed
½ cup chopped onion               with
1 pound ground lamb            1½ teaspoons salt
½ cup boiling water             ⅛ teaspoon pepper
1 cup canned tomatoes           ½ teaspoon powdered
1-1½ tablespoons chili             cumin, if desired
  powder                        2 No. 2 cans kidney beans
2 tablespoons cold water          or
                                4 cups cooked chili beans,
                                  undrained

In hot fat in large skillet, cook onion until tender. Add ground lamb. Cook uncovered until meat starts to sizzle and brown. Add boiling water, tomatoes, chili powder (amount depends upon your taste—better start with 1 tablespoon) mixed with the cold water until smooth, salt

and garlic, pepper and cumin. Simmer, covered, for 1 hour.
Add beans. Simmer ½ hour more. Add a little hot water if
mixture thickens up too much.


## EASY LAMB SOUP

(8 servings)

1 pound ground lamb
¼ teaspoon celery salt
½ teaspoon basil
¼ teaspoon onion salt
Pepper to taste

¼ teaspoon lamb herbs (rosemary, dry mint leaves,
   grated orange rind)
¾ teaspoon paprika
2 2⅛-ounce packages
   dehydrated chicken
   noodle soup mix

Combine lamb, celery salt, basil, onion salt, pepper and
lamb herbs; mix well. Shape into 1½-inch balls. Sprinkle
with paprika. Cook over low heat until browned on all
sides. Drain on absorbent paper. Prepare soup mix according to directions on package. Add lamb and cook over low
heat 30 minutes.


## LAMB VEGETABLE SOUP

(6 to 8 servings)

2 tablespoons butter or
   margarine
1 pound finely chopped
   lamb shoulder
1 cup chopped celery
3 medium-sized onions,
   finely chopped
1 cup cut green beans

1 cup grated carrots
1 cup peas
1 cup shredded cabbage
1 cup lima beans
2 quarts water
   Salt and pepper to taste
½ cup grated Parmesan
   cheese

Melt butter or margarine; add lamb and cook until browned on all sides. Add celery, onions, green beans, carrots, peas, cabbage, lima beans, water and salt and pepper. Cover and cook over low heat 1 hour, stirring occasionally. Serve topped with cheese.

## LAMB SOUP WITH CHIVES

(6 servings)

| | |
|---|---|
| 1 pound lean ground lamb | 1 teaspoon salt |
| 1 medium-sized apple, cored and grated | ⅛ teaspoon pepper |
| | 1 quart water |
| ½ cup sliced scallions | 1 cup light cream |
| ¼ cup all-purpose flour | ¼ cup chopped chives |

Cook lamb over low heat until browned, stirring occasionally. Add apple, scallions, flour, salt and pepper; blend. Gradually add water and cream and cook over low heat, stirring constantly, 5 minutes. Cover and cook 30 minutes. Serve topped with chives.

## JIFFY LAMB ONION SOUP

(8 servings)

| | |
|---|---|
| 1 pound lean ground lamb | ⅛ teaspoon pepper |
| ¼ cup fine dry bread crumbs | 2 10¾-ounce cans condensed onion soup |
| ¼ teaspoon rosemary | 2 cups water |
| ¼ teaspoon celery salt | |

Combine lamb, bread crumbs, rosemary, celery salt and pepper; mix well. Shape into 1½-inch balls. Cook lamb over low heat until browned on all sides. Drain off drippings. Combine onion soup and water. Cook over low heat to boiling point. Add lamb and cook, covered, 30 minutes.

# ROASTS

*To be a true roast, meat should be placed on a rack in an open pan. No water should be added and the pan should not be covered.*

*Don't be afraid to use glazes and sauces as herein indicated, however. These variations will add flavor variety and gourmet appeal, and even though the basting process is not a part of ordinary roasting procedure, the end results will be worthwhile. All recipes for large lamb cuts usually prepared by roasting are included in this section whether dry roasted or basted with sauces and glazes.*

▪▪▪▪▪▪▪▪▪▪▪▪▪▪▪▪▪▪▪▪▪▪▪▪▪▪▪▪▪▪▪▪▪▪▪▪▪▪▪▪▪▪▪▪▪▪

## CRANBERRY LEMON GLAZED LAMB

(6 to 8 servings)

1 4-pound leg of lamb
Salt
1 1-pound can whole
   cranberry sauce

1 tablespoon grated lemon
   rind
¼ cup lemon juice
¾ teaspoon lamb herbs

Sprinkle lamb with salt. Place on rack in roasting pan. Bake in slow oven (300°) 2 hours. Combine remaining ingredients; mix well. Spread over lamb. Bake 1 to 2 hours more, or until meat thermometer registers 170°–180° (depending upon desired degree of doneness). Baste occasionally during baking period.

## CHIVE BAKED LAMB ROAST

(6 servings)

| | |
|---|---|
| 1 5-pound leg of lamb | 2 tablespoons prepared |
| ¼ cup chopped chives | mustard |
| ½ cup lemon juice | ¾ teaspoon rosemary |
| | Salt and pepper |

Place lamb on rack in roasting pan. Bake at 300° F. 2 hours. Combine chives, lemon juice, mustard and rosemary; mix well. Pour over lamb. Sprinkle with salt and pepper. Bake 1 to 2 hours more, or until meat thermometer registers 170°–180° (depending upon desired degree of doneness).

## HONEY-MUSTARD GLAZED LAMB

(6 servings)

| | |
|---|---|
| 1 5-pound leg of lamb | 1 teaspoon salt |
| ½ cup prepared mustard | ¼ teaspoon pepper |
| ½ cup honey | |

Place lamb on rack in shallow roasting pan. Bake in slow oven (300°) 2 hours. Combine remaining ingredients; blend. Pour over lamb. Bake 1 to 2 hours more, or until meat thermometer registers 170°–180° (depending upon desired degree of doneness).

## ITALIAN LEG OF LAMB AND SPAGHETTI
(4 to 6 servings)

1 5-pound leg of lamb
Salt
4 medium-sized onions,
   chopped
1 medium-sized green pepper,
   chopped

1 clove garlic, finely chopped
2 1-pound cans tomatoes
1 medium-sized chili pepper,
   chopped (optional)
8 ounces spaghetti
Grated Parmesan cheese

Place lamb on rack in shallow roasting pan. Sprinkle with salt. Bake in slow oven (300°) 1 hour. Combine onions, green pepper, garlic, tomatoes and chili pepper; mix well. Pour over lamb. Bake 2 to 3 hours more or until meat thermometer registers 170°–180° (depending upon desired degree of doneness). Baste lamb frequently during baking period. Cook spaghetti in boiling salted water. Drain in colander. Place lamb on serving platter. Top spaghetti with tomato mixture. Serve Parmesan cheese with spaghetti.

## LEG OF LAMB WITH MINT-MERINGUE PEARS
(8 to 10 servings)

1 5- to 6-pound leg of lamb
Salt and pepper
8-10 canned Bartlett pear
   halves, or fresh halves
   peeled and cored

2 egg whites
½ cup mint jelly

Do not have the fell removed. Season with salt and pepper. Place skin side down on a rack in an open roasting pan. Insert meat thermometer so bulb reaches center of the thick round of the leg, being sure the thermometer does not rest on bone or fat. Do not add water and do not cover. Roast in a slow oven (300°) until the meat thermometer registers 170°–180° F., depending upon your taste. Serve with mint-meringue pear halves made as follows: Beat egg whites until stiff. Add mint jelly and continue beating until well mixed. Put mint-meringue on cut surface of each pear half and place in oven or broiler just long enough for the meringue to become lightly browned. Serve hot.

## HERB-FLAVORED LEG OF LAMB

### (8 to 10 servings)

| | |
|---|---|
| 1 6- to 8-pound leg of lamb | ½ teaspoon basil |
| 4 slices dry bread * | 1 teaspoon salt |
| 1 teaspoon thyme | ¼ teaspoon pepper |

* Or 1½ cups fine dry bread crumbs. Do not sieve.

Place lamb on rack in roasting pan. Bake in slow oven (300°) 3 hours. Meanwhile, force bread through sieve or food mill. Add remaining ingredients and mix well. Spread over lamb. Bake 30 minutes to 1 hour, or until meat thermometer registers 170°–180°.

## ORANGE MINT-GLAZED LEG OF LAMB

### (6 servings)

| | |
|---|---|
| 1 5-pound leg of lamb | 1 teaspoon rosemary |
| 1 teaspoon salt | ½ cup orange juice |
| ¼ teaspoon pepper | ½ cup chopped mint |

Place lamb on rack in roasting pan. Sprinkle with salt, pepper, and rosemary. Bake in slow oven (300°) 2½ hours. Pour orange juice over lamb. Top with mint. Bake 30 minutes to 1 hour, or until meat thermometer registers 170°–180° (depending upon desired degree of doneness). Baste lamb frequently during baking period. Garnish with additional mint as desired.


## EASTER ROAST LEG OF LAMB

**(8 servings)**

1 8-pound leg of lamb
    Salt and pepper
1 1-pound 4-ounce can sliced
    pineapple, drained
2 medium-sized bananas, cut
    in ½-inch slices

1 cup seeded red grapes
1 medium-sized unpeeled apple, cored and cut in wedges

Place lamb on rack in shallow roasting pan. Sprinkle with salt and pepper. Bake in slow oven (300°) 3½ hours. Drain off drippings. Add remaining ingredients. Bake 30 to 60 minutes or until meat thermometer registers 170°–180° (depending upon desired degree of doneness).


## GLAZED FRENCH RACK OF LAMB

**(4 servings)**

1 3-pound French rack of
    lamb
    Salt and pepper
½ cup orange marmalade

⅓ cup lemon juice
1 teaspoon rosemary
¼ cup finely chopped parsley

Sprinkle lamb with salt and pepper. Place on rack in roasting pan. Bake in slow oven (300°) 1½ hours. Combine remaining

ingredients; blend. Spread over lamb. Bake 30 minutes to 1
hour, or until meat thermometer registers 170°–180° (depending upon desired degree of doneness).

## CROWN ROAST

In ordering, allow two ribs per serving and ask that ends of
rib bones be "Frenched" (meat removed from ends of rib
bones). Sprinkle crown roast all over with salt and pepper.
Garlic salt may also be used, if desired. Place, ribs down,
in uncovered shallow pan. Insert meat thermometer between
ribs into center of thickest part of meat, being sure it does
not rest in fat or touch bone. Wrap stuffing in heavy aluminum foil, using drugstore wrap to keep stuffing moist. Place
in a separate shallow pan. Place crown roast and stuffing in
300° F. oven. Cook until meat thermometer reaches 170°–
172° for medium done, 180° for well done. Roasting time
will be approximately 2½ hours. About ½ hour before lamb
is done, remove from oven. Pour fat from pan. Turn roast
rib ends up. Remove stuffing from foil and fill cavity. Return
to oven and finish roasting.

### Stuffing

½ cup butter
½ cup minced onion
¾-1 cup finely cut celery
3 tablespoons minced
parsley, if desired
2 quarts (8 cups) cubes
from day-old bread

¾ pound (1½ cups) lean
ground lamb from
trimmings
¾ teaspoon salt
⅛ teaspoon pepper
½ teaspoon powdered
thyme
*or* poultry seasoning

Melt butter in large skillet. Add onion and celery and simmer
until tender but not browned. Using a slotted spoon or

turner, lift onion and celery onto bread cubes. Pour on most of the melted butter. Add parsley. Using a fork, mix in lightly. Add lamb to butter in skillet. Cook until lamb begins to brown, breaking it up with fork in small pieces. Add seasonings. Cool slightly, then mix lightly into the onion-bread mixture. Place on a large piece of heavy aluminum foil, or two pieces, criss-crossed, of the lighter-weight foil. Wrap carefully to insure a good seal. See roasting directions for use with Crown Roast, above.

## CROWN ROAST OF LAMB

(6 to 8 servings)

| | |
|---|---|
| ½ cup butter or margarine | 1 teaspoon salt |
| ½ pound mushrooms | ¼ teaspoon pepper |
| ½ cup chopped onion | 1 5-pound crown roast of |
| ½ cup chopped celery | lamb |
| 3 cups soft bread cubes | |

Melt butter or margarine; add mushrooms, onions and celery. Cook until tender, stirring occasionally. Add crumbs, salt and pepper; mix well. Place lamb on rack in shallow roasting pan. Fill with mushroom mixture. Bake in slow oven (300°) 3 to 3¾ hours, or until meat thermometer registers 170°–180° (depending upon desired degree of doneness).

*Note:* Thermometer should be inserted between ribs in thickest part of meat, making sure it does not rest in fat or against bone.

## CURRANT-GLAZED LAMB SHOULDER ROAST

(About 8 servings)

1 boned shoulder of lamb,     ¾ cup currant jelly
    rolled and tied     ¼ cup water
2 tablespoons all-purpose     8 medium-sized carrots, cut
    flour        in half
1 teaspoon salt     16 small white onions
¼ teaspoon pepper

Place lamb on rack in shallow roasting pan. Bake in slow oven (300°) 1 hour. Combine flour, salt, pepper, jelly and water; blend. Spread on lamb. Arrange vegetables on rack with lamb. Bake in slow oven (300°) 1½ to 2 hours, or until meat thermometer registers 170°–180° (depending upon desired degree of doneness). Baste vegetables occasionally during baking period.

## MARMALADE-GLAZED LAMB SHOULDER

(8 servings)

1 shoulder of lamb, boned,     ¼ teaspoon pepper
    rolled and tied     ¾ cup orange marmalade
2 tablespoons all-purpose     ¼ cup lemon juice
    flour        ¼ cup chopped parsley
1 teaspoon salt

Place lamb on rack in shallow roasting pan. Bake in slow oven (300°) 1½ hours. Combine flour, salt, pepper, marmalade and lemon juice; blend. Spread on lamb. Sprinkle with parsley. Bake 1½ to 2 hours, or until meat thermometer registers 170°–180°.

## SWEET AND SOUR SHOULDER OF LAMB

(8 servings)

| | |
|---|---|
| 1 boneless shoulder of lamb, rolled and tied | ½ teaspoon salt |
| | 3 tablespoons brown sugar |
| ¾ cup cider vinegar | 1 medium-sized onion, sliced |
| ¾ cup water | 2 sprigs parsley |

Place lamb on rack in roasting pan. Combine vinegar, water, salt, sugar, onion and parsley; mix well. Pour over lamb. Bake in slow oven (300°) 3 to 4 hours or until meat thermometer registers 170°–180°. Baste lamb frequently during baking period.

## GRAPE-BAKED SHOULDER OF LAMB

(6 to 8 servings)

| | |
|---|---|
| 1 boned shoulder of lamb, rolled and tied | ¾ cup currant jelly |
| | 2 cups seeded grapes |
| Salt and pepper | 1 tablespoon grated lemon rind |
| ½ cup lemon juice | |

Sprinkle lamb with salt and pepper. Place on rack in roasting pan. Bake in slow oven (300°) 2 hours. Combine remaining ingredients; mix well. Pour over lamb. Bake until meat thermometer registers 170°–180° (depending upon desired degree of doneness). Baste lamb with grape mixture frequently during baking period.

## OVEN-POACHED ROLLED LAMB SHOULDER

(6 servings)

1 rolled, boned shoulder of
lamb, coated with the
following:
3/4 stick of butter ( 6
tablespoons )
2 smallish cloves of garlic,
minced *or*
1/2 teaspoon garlic salt

1 tablespoon flour
1 1/2 teaspoons salt
2 teaspoons monosodium
glutamate
1/4 teaspoon coarse-ground
pepper
1 tablespoon lemon juice
1 cup currant or mint jelly

Cream together thoroughly all ingredients except jelly.
Spread this all over the lamb. Place coated lamb, with the
bones alongside, on a big piece of aluminum foil. Draw surface edges together using a drugstore fold, then fold up and
crimp ends of foil leaving enough room for juice which
collects during baking. Double-wrap by placing the package on another piece of foil, going the other way. Seal. This
may be prepared early in the morning, or, better still, the
day before. A few hours in the refrigerator adds flavor. To
cook, place foil-wrapped packet in a shallow pan in an oven
heated to 375°. Allow 35 minutes to the pound for medium,
40 to 45 for well done. The foil serves as a cover, hence an
oven temperature higher than the conventional roasting
temperature is used. A meat thermometer interferes with
the foil packaging. When the time is almost up, remove
lamb from foil and place on heatproof platter or shallow
pan. Discard bones and pour the juice into a skillet or
saucepan. Melt 1 cup currant or mint jelly over low heat,
stirring all the time. Remove strings from roast. Slash deeply
into the roast, and drizzle the melted jelly over the surface
and into the slashes. Return to the oven to glaze while you
make the gravy.

*Gravy:*

Add water, if necessary, to the juice to make 2 cups. Mix together 4 teaspoons cornstarch and ½ cup cold water. Stir into the hot juice and cook until thickened, stirring constantly. Serve piping hot. Roast lamb is usually served in ¼-inch to ⅜-inch slices. This style of lamb may be served in ½-inch slices if desired. If served cold, slice thin.

## LAMB SHOULDER ROAST WITH FRUIT

### (6 to 8 servings)

1 boneless shoulder of lamb, rolled and tied
Salt and pepper
½ teaspoon rosemary
1 1-pound 13-ounce can whole apricots

1 1-pound 13-ounce can peach halves, drained
½ cup seedless red grapes, cut in half
¼ cup chopped mint

Place lamb on rack in shallow roasting pan. Sprinkle with salt and pepper and rosemary. Bake in slow oven (300°) 2½ hours. Drain apricots; reserve sirup. Arrange peach halves around lamb; top with apricots, grapes and mint. Pour apricot sirup over lamb and fruit. Bake 30 minutes, or until meat thermometer registers 170°–180° (depending upon desired degree of doneness). Baste with apricot sirup frequently during baking period.

## LAMB SHOULDER WITH VEGETABLES, ARMENIAN

### (6 to 8 servings)

Square-cut style lamb shoulder
Carrots
Potatoes
Eggplant
Onions

Zucchini, if desired
Fresh or canned whole
    tomatoes
Parsley, bay leaf
Garlic clove, if desired

Lamb shoulder, square-cut with bone in, will usually weigh 4 to 5 pounds. Allow ½ to ¾ pound bone-in shoulder roast per serving. Place prepared whole vegetables and quartered eggplant in roaster. Sprinkle with salt and pepper, parsley; add bay leaf. Sprinkle meaty side of lamb with salt and pepper. If desired, rub lamb all over with cut garlic clove or insert slivers of garlic in lamb. Place lamb, skin side up, on top of vegetables and cover with tight-fitting lid. (If using canned solid-pack tomatoes instead of fresh, use only the solid portions.) Cut celery or celery tops may be placed on vegetables. Place covered pan in 375° oven and cook for about 2 hours or until lamb is fork-tender. Remove lid of roaster and allow meat to remain in oven for approximately 30 minutes more to lightly brown top (skin side) of lamb. Place lamb on heated platter or on a carving board. Arrange vegetables in shallow bowl. The liquid in the pan may be poured over the vegetables or thickened with a bit of flour and used as a gravy.

In serving, this type of roast should be cut from the bones in chunks. Because of the large flat bone inside the roast, it does not slice well.

*Note:* The moisture from vegetables and use of covered roaster make it desirable to use a temperature higher than usual for roasting above.

## GLAZED LAMB SHOULDER WITH
## ORANGE MINT SAUCE

(About 8 servings)

1 4-pound boned shoulder of
    lamb, rolled and tied
1 6-ounce can frozen orange
    juice concentrate
¼ cup lemon juice
¼ cup butter or margarine

½ teaspoon salt
½ cup finely chopped celery
¼ cup slivered almonds
¼ cup chopped mint *or*
2 tablespoons
    dehydrated mint flakes

Place lamb on rack in shallow roasting pan. Bake in slow oven (300°) 1¼ hours. Combine orange juice concentrate, lemon juice, butter or margarine and salt. Cook 5 minutes; mix well. Brush lamb with orange juice mixture. Bake 1½ to 2 hours, or until meat thermometer registers 170°–180° (depending upon desired degree of doneness). Brush occasionally with orange juice mixture during baking period. Meanwhile, combine remaining orange juice mixture and celery. Cook 5 minutes. Add almonds and mint or mint flakes; mix well. Serve with lamb.

## ONION-STUFFED LAMB SHOULDER

(6 to 8 servings)

¼ cup butter or margarine
1 tablespoon paprika
3 cups sliced onions
1 teaspoon salt
¼ teaspoon pepper

2 cups soft bread crumbs
1 6-pound shoulder of lamb,
    cut for stuffing
Salt and pepper

Melt butter or margarine; add paprika and mix well. Add onions and cook until tender, stirring occasionally. Add 1 teaspoon salt, ¼ teaspoon pepper and crumbs; mix well. Fill lamb with onion mixture. Sprinkle with salt and pepper. Place on rack in shallow roasting pan. Bake in slow oven

(300°) 3 to 3½ hours, or until meat thermometer registers 170°–180° (depending upon desired degree of doneness).

## CUSHION SHOULDER OF LAMB WITH PRUNE STUFFING

(8 servings)

1 cushion-style lamb shoulder, scored
1 teaspoon salt
1 small lemon
3 tablespoons butter or margarine
1 medium-sized onion, chopped
1 cup diced celery
1 cup prepared stuffing mix
3 cups dried prunes, cooked and pitted
½ cup chopped walnuts
½ teaspoon salt
2 tablespoons chopped mint

Sprinkle lamb pocket with 1 teaspoon salt. Slice half of lemon. Chop remaining lemon. Melt butter or margarine; add onion and celery and cook 5 minutes. Add chopped lemon, stuffing mix, prunes, walnuts and ½ teaspoon salt. Mix well. Arrange stuffing mixture in pocket of lamb. Fasten with string or skewers. Top with lemon slices and mint. Bake in slow oven (300°) about 2½ hours.

## ROAST CUSHION OF LAMB WITH APPLE-MINT STUFFING

1 cushion-style lamb shoulder (boned, to form a pocket)
Salt and pepper to season
2½-3 cups small cubes of day-old bread
¾ cup coarsely chopped, peeled tart apples
½ cup small celery pieces
¼ cup butter
¼ cup snipped fresh mint leaves or
1 teaspoon dry mint leaves
½ teaspoon salt
⅛ teaspoon pepper

Have a square-cut lamb shoulder boned to leave a pocket for stuffing. Allow ¼ to ⅓ pound boned roast per serving. Sprinkle the boned lamb shoulder inside and out with salt and pepper. Combine bread cubes with the apple, celery cooked gently in the butter, mint leaves, and seasonings. Fill the shoulder pocket with the stuffing. (We like to double the stuffing recipe, wrap it in aluminum foil and bake it the last half of the cooking time for the roast. It's so good someone will want an extra portion over and above what was pocketed in the lamb.) Sew the opening, or, using skewers or poultry pins set at right angles through the open part, lace back and forth with string as if lacing a shoe. Place skin or "fell" side up in open pan. If desired, score the surface with a sharp knife, by cutting through the skin uniformly about ⅛ inch deep to form diamond shapes. Rub a lemon half over the surface, squeezing gently so that the juice goes into the cut portions. Roast in a 300° oven for about 2½ to 3 hours. Serve hot on a heated platter and do have hot plates.

## CUSHION SHOULDER ROAST OF LAMB WITH PRUNE-ORANGE STUFFING

(8 servings)

1 4-pound cushion shoulder roast of lamb
Salt, 1 teaspoon for each pound of meat
1 tablespoon finely chopped onion
¼ cup butter
6 cups half-inch bread cubes
¾ cup orange sections, cut in thirds (1½ small oranges)
1 cup cut, cooked, pitted prunes
¾ teaspoon ground oregano
½ teaspoon salt
⅛ teaspoon ground black pepper

*Apricot Stuffing*

6 cups soft bread cubes,        1⅓ cups dried apricots (cut
   small                               in small pieces)
¾ teaspoon salt                 ½ cup minced onion
¼ teaspoon pepper               1 cup chopped celery
¼ teaspoon powdered thyme       ⅓ cup melted butter
   *or* poultry seasoning

Ask your meat dealer to remove the fell (outside covering) and crack the bones of the breast so it can be carved easily between the ribs when served. Have a pocket made in the breast by cutting through the flesh close to the ribs. Rub the inside of pocket and outside with salt and pepper; use a little lemon or garlic if you wish additional seasoning. Prepare bread cubes. Add seasonings. Place apricots in a saucepan and cover with a little water. Cover; when water is boiling, remove from heat and let stand about a minute, or until apricots are slightly tender. Drain off liquid. Cook onions and celery in the melted butter over low heat, until tender but not browned. Add to bread mixture along with the apricots. Fill lamb pocket with Apricot Stuffing and fasten opening with skewers, or poultry pins and string, as you would a turkey—lacing shoestring fashion. Place breast —ribs down—in a shallow baking dish. Cook in 300° oven about 2¼ hours, or until tender.

## SHERRIED BREAST OF LAMB

**(4 servings)**

1 breast of lamb (about 2       1 clove garlic, finely chopped
   pounds)                          2 tablespoons finely chopped
1 8-ounce can tomato sauce         onion
½ cup dry sherry                2 tablespoons soy sauce
½ cup honey

Place lamb on rack in shallow pan. Bake in moderate oven
(350°) 40 minutes. Drain off drippings. Combine tomato
sauce, sherry, honey, garlic, onion and soy sauce. Pour over
lamb. Reduce heat to 300°. Bake until tender (approximately 1½ to 2 hours), basting frequently with sherry mixture.

cranberry glaze over ring and pile center high with buttered peas.

### Cranberry Glaze

1 1-pound can whole cran-        2 tablespoons fresh lemon
  berry sauce                      juice
½ cup brown sugar

Break up cranberry sauce with fork. Add sugar and lemon juice and stir together. Heat. Spoon over lamb ring just before serving.

## LAMB LOAVES WITH CURRIED PEAS

(4 servings)

1 pound ground lamb              1 teaspoon salt
1 tablespoon minced onion          Few grains pepper
    or 1 tablespoon dry          ¼ cup fine dry bread crumbs
    shredded green onion         ⅔ cup evaporated milk

Place all ingredients in a medium-sized mixing bowl and mix together thoroughly with a fork. Shape meat mixture into four rectangular loaves and place in a shallow baking pan. Bake in preheated moderate oven (350° F.) until loaves are done and lightly browned, about 40 minutes. Serve hot with curried peas.

### Curried Peas

1 package frozen peas (10        2 tablespoons flour
  ounces)                        1 teaspoon curry powder
2 tablespoons butter             1 cup evaporated milk

Using ½ cup water and ½ teaspoon salt, cook peas according to package directions. While peas are cooking, melt butter in saucepan. Add flour and curry powder, stirring to blend thoroughly. Drain peas, saving liquid. (There should be about ⅓ cup liquid. If not, add water to make that amount.) Gradually add liquid from peas to the flour mixture and stir constantly over low heat until mixture is thickened. Add milk, a little at a time, stirring constantly to keep smooth. Stir in peas and serve at once over lamb loaves.

*Note:* One can of peas (No. 303) may be substituted for the frozen peas. Do not cook, but drain peas and use ⅓ cup of the liquid in making the sauce as directed above.

## LAMB PINEAPPLE LOAF

**(4 servings)**

1 pound ground lamb
1 cup packaged bread
    stuffing
1 9-ounce can pineapple
    tidbits

1 egg, beaten
¾ teaspoon salt
Pepper to taste

Combine all ingredients; mix well. Press into 9x5x3-inch loaf pan. Bake in a slow oven (300°) about 1¼ hours. Drain off drippings.

## CURRIED HAWAIIAN LAMB SPARERIBS

**(4 servings)**

3 pounds lamb spareribs
1 teaspoon curry powder
1 teaspoon salt
¼ teaspoon pepper
⅓ cup finely chopped celery
¼ cup chopped parsley
1 teaspoon grated lemon
    rind

1 cup orange juice
1 medium-sized orange,
    sliced
1 medium-sized lemon, sliced
1 medium-sized pineapple,
    pared, cored and sliced *

\* Or 1-pound 4-ounce can sliced pineapple, drained.

Place spareribs on rack in shallow roasting pan. Bake at 325° F. about 1½ hours. Drain off drippings. Combine curry powder, salt, pepper, celery, parsley, lemon rind and orange juice; mix well. Pour over spareribs. Top with orange, lemon and pineapple slices. Bake 45 minutes longer, or until completely tender. Baste lamb frequently during baking period.

## LAMB RIBS, CHINESE STYLE

(4 servings)

2½-3 pounds lamb breast, cut in four pieces
½ cup soy sauce
¼ cup water
1½ tablespoons sherry

1 teaspoon sugar
1 clove garlic, mashed with
½ teaspoon salt

Slice through meat between the ribs without cutting all the way through. Combine the remaining ingredients and let ribs stand in this mixture for 1 or 2 hours under refrigeration; turn once. Remove ribs and place in a shallow baking pan in a hot oven (425°) for 15 to 20 minutes. Pour off fat, then reduce heat to 325° and continue baking 1 hour or until fork-tender, basting frequently with the soy sauce mixture.

## STUFFED LAMB CHOP SPECIAL

(4 servings)

¼ cup butter or margarine
½ cup chopped onion
¼ cup chopped mushrooms
½ cup chopped celery
1 cup soft bread crumbs
¼ cup chopped parsley
2 canned pimientos, chopped

1 bay leaf, crumbled
1 teaspoon paprika
1 teaspoon salt
¼ teaspoon pepper
4 double-rib lamp chops, cut for stuffing

Melt butter or margarine; add onion, mushrooms and celery. Cook until tender, stirring occasionally. Add crumbs, parsley, pimientos, bay leaf, paprika, salt and pepper; mix well. Fill chops with crumb mixture. Place in shallow baking pan. Bake in slow oven (300°) 1½ hours, or to desired degree of doneness.

## LAMB SAUERKRAUT BAKE

(4 servings)

| | |
|---|---|
| 1 1-pound can sauerkraut | 1 teaspoon caraway seeds |
| 1 1-pound 4-ounce can tomatoes | 1 2-pound breast of lamb |

Arrange undrained kraut in shallow baking dish; add tomatoes and caraway seeds. Top with lamb. Bake at 350° 1½ hours, or until tender.

## LAMB STEAKS IN WINE

(4 servings)

| | |
|---|---|
| 1 clove garlic, cut in half | 3 tablespoons chopped scallions |
| 2 lamb leg steaks, about ½ inch thick | 1 tablespoon chopped parsley |
| 1 teaspoon salt | 1½ tablespoons all-purpose flour |
| ¼ teaspoon pepper | ½ cup dry white wine |
| 2 tablespoons salad oil | |
| ¼ cup chopped dry onion | |

Rub garlic on lamb; sprinkle with salt and pepper. Heat oil in heavy skillet; add lamb and cook until lightly browned on both sides. Place lamb in shallow baking dish; reserve drippings. Cook onion, scallions and parsley in drippings until onion is tender. Stir in flour and gradually add wine; cook until thickened, stirring constantly. Pour over lamb. Cover and bake at 350° F., 20 minutes or until tender. Uncover and bake 10 minutes more.

## LAMB NECK VEGETABLE CASSEROLE

(4 servings)

1 1-pound can cream-style corn
1 1-pound can lima beans, drained
2 medium-sized tomatoes, diced
¾ teaspoon salt
⅛ teaspoon pepper
4 lamb neck slices, ¾ inch thick

Combine corn, lima beans, tomatoes, salt and pepper; mix well. Arrange 2 lamb neck slices in bottom of 2-quart casserole. Pour corn mixture on top. Top with remaining neck slices. Bake at 325° F. 45 minutes, or until tender.

## BREAST OF LAMB WITH APPLES

(4 servings)

1 2-pound breast of lamb
1 teaspoon cloves
⅛ teaspoon nutmeg
1 tablespoon brown sugar
1 teaspoon salt
¼ teaspoon pepper
1 teaspoon onion salt
1 1-pound 4-ounce can sliced apples

Place lamb on rack in baking pan. Bake in slow oven (300°) 1 hour. Combine cloves, nutmeg, sugar, salt, pepper and onion salt; mix well. Spread over lamb. Top with apples. Bake 1 hour, or until tender.

## BREAST OF LAMB WITH SOUR CREAM TOPPING

**(4 servings)**

| | |
|---|---|
| 3 pounds breast of lamb | ½ teaspoon dehydrated |
| 1 cup commercial sour cream | parsley flakes |
| ¼ teaspoon rosemary | ½ teaspoon onion salt |
| | Pepper to taste |

Place lamb on rack in shallow roasting pan. Bake in slow oven (300°) 1 hour 45 minutes, or until tender. Drain off drippings. Combine remaining ingredients; mix well. Spread over lamb. Bake 15 minutes.

## BAKED LAMB STUFFED TOMATOES

**(4 servings)**

| | |
|---|---|
| 4 medium-sized tomatoes, cut in half | ½ teaspoon salt |
| | Pepper to taste |
| ¾ pound ground lamb | ¼ cup grated Cheddar |
| 3 tablespoons chopped onion | cheese |
| ½ teaspoon ground basil | |

Scoop out pulp from tomatoes. Combine lamb, tomato pulp, onion, basil, salt and pepper; mix well. Fill tomatoes with lamb mixture. Top with cheese. Place in shallow baking pan. Bake at 325° F. 45 minutes.

## WESTERN LAMB SPARERIBS

(4 servings)

3 pounds lamb spareribs        1 medium-sized onion, sliced
1 6-ounce can tomato paste     1 teaspoon salt
½ cup catchup                  ¼ teaspoon pepper
¼ cup vinegar                  Dash Tabasco sauce
¼ cup molasses

Place spareribs on rack in shallow roasting pan. Bake at
325° F. approximately 1½ hours. Drain off drippings. Combine remaining ingredients; mix well. Pour over spareribs.
Bake 45 minutes, or until tender. Baste lamb frequently with
tomato paste mixture during baking period.

## PINEAPPLE BARBECUED LAMB SPARERIBS

(4 servings)

3 pounds lamb spareribs        1 teaspoon Worcestershire
1 8-ounce can crushed             sauce
   pineapple                   1 teaspoon salt
¼ cup vinegar                  ⅛ teaspoon pepper
¼ cup honey                    ¼ teaspoon ginger
1 clove garlic, finely chopped

Place spareribs on rack in shallow roasting pan. Bake at
325° F. approximately 1½ hours. Drain off drippings. Combine remaining ingredients; mix well. Pour over lamb. Bake
45 minutes, or until tender. Baste lamb with pineapple mixture frequently during baking period.

## LAMB STEAKS AND VEGETABLES

(4 servings)

2 lamb steaks, about ½ inch
  thick
2 cloves garlic, finely
  chopped
1 cup sliced mushrooms
1 cup chopped green pepper
1 cup chopped onion

2 medium-sized tomatoes,
  sliced
1 teaspoon salt
¼ teaspoon pepper
2 teaspoons paprika
½ teaspoon rosemary
¼ cup dry sherry

Arrange lamb in shallow baking dish. Top with sliced to-
matoes. Combine remaining ingredients; spread over meat.
Bake at 325° F. 40 minutes, or to desired degree of doneness.
Baste lamb frequently during baking period.

## STUFFED LAMB CHOPS

(4 servings)

2 tablespoons butter or
  margarine
2 tablespoons finely chopped
  onion
½ cup finely chopped celery
2 cups soft bread crumbs

½ teaspoon poultry seasoning
Salt and pepper to taste
¼ cup milk
4 double-rib lamb chops, cut
  for stuffing
Paprika

Melt butter or margarine; add onion and celery and sauté
until tender. Add bread crumbs, poultry seasoning, salt and
pepper and milk; mix well. Fill chops with bread mixture;
sprinkle with paprika. Place on rack in shallow baking pan.
Bake in slow oven (300°) 1½ hours, or to desired degree of
doneness.

## OVEN-BARBECUE LAMB RIBLETS

(8 servings)

2 rib sections from breast of          1 lemon, thinly sliced
   lamb                                 Salt and pepper
4 medium onions, sliced                Smoked salt, if desired

Have two rib sections of breast of lamb trimmed and cut in
2-rib portions. Brown on both sides over moderate heat, or
in hot oven. Drain off drippings. Arrange lamb in roaster
with tight-fitting cover. Sprinkle lightly with salt, pepper
and a bit of smoked salt, if desired. Tuck in between lamb,
the onion and lemon slices. Combine ingredients for sauce,
using recipe below. Pour over lamb. Cover tightly. Bake at
325° for 1½ hours, or until fork-tender. Spoon sauce over
ribs two or three times during this period, adding a bit of
water if necessary to keep sauce from sticking to pan. Uncover and bake 15 to 20 minutes more.


### Barbecue Sauce

Combine and pour over browned lamb:

1 cup catchup                          Several dashes Tabasco
1 cup water                              sauce
¼ cup vinegar                          2 teaspoons dry mustard
2 tablespoons sugar                    Clove of garlic mashed or
4 teaspoons Worcestershire               minced with 2 teaspoons
  sauce                                   salt

## LAMB LASAGNA

(6 to 8 servings)

1½ pounds ground lamb
1 cup chopped onion
1 clove garlic, finely
   chopped
2 1-pound 4-ounce cans
   tomatoes
1 6-ounce can tomato paste
2 teaspoons salt
¼ teaspoon pepper

½ teaspoon oregano
¼ teaspoon rosemary
1 pound lasagna noodles
1 cup creamed cottage
   cheese
½ pound Mozzarella cheese,
   sliced
½ cup grated Parmesan
   cheese

Combine lamb, onions and garlic; cook until lightly browned, stirring occasionally. Add tomatoes, tomato paste, 2 teaspoons salt, pepper, oregano and rosemary. Cover and cook over low heat 1 hour, stirring occasionally. Cook lasagna uncovered, in boiling salted water, stirring occasionally, until tender. Drain in colander. Arrange layers of lamb mixture, lasagna and cheeses in shallow 3-quart baking dish. Bake at 350° F. 1 hour.

## ITALIAN LAMB NECK SLICES

(4 servings)

4 lamb neck slices, about
   ¾ inch thick
1 8-ounce can tomato sauce
⅓ cup chopped green pepper
1 tablespoon chopped onion

¼ teaspoon lamb herbs (rosemary, dry mint leaves,
   grated orange rind)
½ teaspoon salt
⅛ teaspoon pepper
¼ cup grated Cheddar cheese

Arrange lamb in shallow baking pan. Combine tomato sauce, green pepper, onion, lamb herbs, salt and pepper;

mix well. Pour sauce over lamb and sprinkle with cheese.
Bake at 325° F. 40 minutes, or until tender.


## LAMB PARMIGIANA

(4 servings)

½ cup fine dry bread crumbs
¼ cup grated Parmesan
    cheese
¼ teaspoon lamb herbs (rose-
    mary, dry mint leaves,
    grated orange rind)
4 lamb neck slices, ¾ inch
    thick

1 egg, beaten
3 tablespoons salad oil
1 10½-ounce can meatless
    spaghetti sauce
¼ pound Mozzarella cheese
2 teaspoons grated Parmesan
    cheese

Combine bread crumbs, ¼ cup Parmesan cheese and lamb
herbs; mix well. Dip lamb in egg and coat with bread-crumb
mixture. Heat salad oil. Cook lamb in salad oil until browned
on both sides. Arrange lamb in shallow baking pan. Top
with half of spaghetti sauce. Top each neck slice with a
slice of Mozzarella cheese. Top with remaining spaghetti
sauce. Sprinkle with 2 teaspoons Parmesan cheese. Bake at
325° F. 30 to 40 minutes.


## LAMB AND EGGPLANT BAKE

(6 servings)

⅓ cup butter or margarine
1 medium-sized eggplant,
    sliced lengthwise in ½-
    inch slices
1 pound ground lamb
¼ cup chopped onion
½ teaspoon salt

Dash pepper
1 8-ounce can tomato sauce
¼ cup grated Parmesan
    cheese
½ pound Mozzarella cheese,
    sliced

Melt butter or margarine. Add eggplant slices; cook over low heat until lightly browned on both sides. Place in shallow 2-quart baking pan; reserve drippings. Add lamb, onion, salt and pepper to drippings. Cook until lamb is lightly browned. Place over eggplant. Add tomato sauce and Parmesan cheese. Bake at 350° F. 20 minutes. Add Mozzarella cheese; bake 10 minutes, or until cheese is bubbly and melted.

## BREADED LAMB SHOULDER AND EGGPLANT

(4 servings)

| | |
|---|---|
| ¼ cup milk | der, sliced about ⅛ inch |
| 1 egg, slightly beaten | thick |
| 1 cup fine dry bread crumbs | 1 meduim-sized eggplant, |
| 1 teaspoon paprika | pared and cut in ½-inch |
| 2 teaspoons salt | slices |
| ¼ teaspoon pepper | ¼ cup melted butter or |
| 1 pound boned lamb shoul- | margarine |

Combine milk and egg; blend. Combine bread crumbs, paprika, salt and pepper; blend. Dip lamb and eggplant in egg mixture; coat with crumb mixture. Pour butter or margarine into shallow baking pan; add lamb and eggplant. Bake at 350° F. 1 hour, or until lightly browned and tender. Turn frequently during baking period. Drain on absorbent paper, if desired.

## LAMB-STUFFED EGGPLANT I

**(4 servings)**

1 large eggplant, cut in
   half lengthwise
3 tablespoons salad oil
1 small onion, chopped
1 medium-sized green
   pepper, diced
1½ cups cooked rice

1 1-pound 4-ounce can
   tomatoes
½ teaspoon basil
½ teaspoon garlic salt
2 cups diced cooked lamb
   Salt and pepper to taste

Cut center from eggplant, leaving ½-inch shell; reserve shell.
Dice eggplant pulp. Combine oil, onion, green pepper and
eggplant; sauté until vegetables are tender. Add rice and
cook over low heat, stirring occasionally, until rice is tender.
Add tomatoes, basil and garlic salt; heat to boiling point,
stirring occasionally. Cook over low heat 15 minutes. Add
lamb and salt and pepper; mix well. Fill eggplant shells
with lamb mixture. Place in shallow baking pan. Bake at
350° F. 45 minutes.

## LAMB-STUFFED EGGPLANT II

**(4 servings)**

1 large, firm eggplant
½ cup chopped green onion
   (or 1 small dry onion,
   chopped)
¼ cup chopped green pepper
2 tablespoons butter
1 can (10½ ounces)
   condensed tomato soup

2 cups finely cut roast lamb
1 teaspoon salt
¼ teaspoon pepper
1 cup cooked rice
½ cup shredded
   quick-melting cheese
¼ cup sliced ripe olives, if
   desired

Cut eggplant in half lengthwise, and hollow out all the pulp
to make a ¼-inch-thick shell. Chop the pulp. Cook the onion

and green pepper in the butter in a skillet until they are limp and tender. Add the chopped pulp, tomato soup, lamb, salt, pepper, rice, cheese and olives. Cook and stir about 2 minutes. Spoon half of the mixture into each eggplant shell. Place in a baking pan and bake at 350° F. approximately 45 minutes, or until done.

## HERBED LAMB LOAF

(6 servings)

2 eggs, unbeaten
1¼ pounds ground lamb
¼ pound ground pork
1 cup rolled oats (quick or old-fashioned, uncooked)
¾ cup chicken bouillon (made by dissolving 1 bouillon cube in ¾ cup boiling water)

¼ cup minced onion
1½ teaspoons salt
¼ teaspoon pepper
¼ teaspoon sweet basil
¼ teaspoon oregano
Lemon slices
Melted butter

Heat oven to 350° F. With fork, beat eggs slightly. Lightly mix in the meat, then rolled oats and remaining ingredients. Combine lightly but well. (Meat will be juicier and more tender if you handle it as little as possible.) In bowl, shape meat into an oval loaf. Transfer to shallow baking dish or heatproof platter and smooth into a shapely rectangular loaf. Place slices of lemon brushed with melted butter on top of the loaf. Bake 1 hour in moderate oven. Serve from baking dish or heatproof platter, spooning off the excess juices to make a gravy if desired. Or spoon some of the juices over the loaf. If you prefer a soft, moist exterior, bake lamb loaf as directed in a 9x5x3-inch loaf pan or in a 1½-quart ring mold. Pour juices from pan after baking. Unmold meat loaf onto cake rack. Then place, right side up, on heated platter. If ring mold is used, fill the center with hot buttered or creamed vegetables, and serve with a mixed green salad.

## CARROT LAMB LOAF

### (Makes one 9x5x3-inch loaf)

| | |
|---|---|
| 1½ pounds ground lamb | ¼ cup chopped onion |
| 2 cups grated carrots | 1 teaspoon salt |
| 1½ cups soft bread crumbs | ¼ teaspoon pepper |
| 1 egg, beaten | ¼ cup chopped parsley |
| ½ cup catchup | |

Combine all ingredients and mix well. Press into greased 9x5x3-inch loaf pan. Bake at 350° F. 1½ hours. Pour off drippings. Serve with fluffy curry sauce.

### Fluffy Curry Sauce

### (Makes about 4 cups)

| | |
|---|---|
| ½ cup instant nonfat dry milk crystals | 1½ cups mayonnaise or salad dressing |
| ½ cup ice water | 2 teaspoons curry powder |
| 2 tablespoons lemon juice | |

Mix instant crystals with ice water in bowl. Whip until soft peaks form (3 to 4 minutes). Add lemon juice; continue beating until stiff peaks form (3 to 4 minutes longer). Lightly fold mayonnaise into whipped instant crystals to blend. Add curry powder and blend. Heat in top of double boiler over hot water to serving temperature.

## EASY LAMB LOAF

(6 servings)

2 cups soft bread crumbs
⅔ cup milk
2 eggs, slightly beaten
1 medium-sized onion,
  chopped
1 canned pimiento,
  chopped

½ cup drained sweet pickle
  relish
1½ pounds ground lamb
2 teaspoons salt

Combine all ingredients; mix well. Press into greased 9x5x3-inch loaf pan. Bake at 375° F. 1 hour. Drain off drippings. Turn out on serving platter. Garnish as desired.

## BAKED RICE LAMB LOAF CASSEROLE

(6 to 8 servings)

4 cups cooked rice (1 cup
  uncooked rice, cooked)
1 can (2 ounces) mushroom
  pieces, drained
1 pound ground lamb
1 teaspoon salt
¼ teaspoon pepper

1 tablespoon prepared
  mustard
1 onion, chopped
1 egg
½ cup dry bread crumbs
½ cup milk
¼ teaspoon thyme

Combine rice and mushroom pieces in a 2-quart casserole, lining sides and bottom of dish. Mix together all remaining ingredients and spread over the rice. Bake at 350° F. 45 minutes.

*Note:* This can be done in individual casseroles. Noodles or macaroni can be used instead of rice.

## LAMB CHEESE LOAF

(6 servings)

1½ pounds ground lamb
1 cup grated Cheddar
   cheese (about ¼
   pound)
½ cup sliced scallions
1 cup chopped celery

1 cup fine dry bread crumbs
1 egg, beaten
1 teaspoon salt
¼ teaspoon pepper
1 teaspoon onion salt

Combine all ingredients; mix well. Press into 9x5x3-inch loaf pan. Bake at 350° F. 1 hour. Drain off drippings.

## INDIVIDUAL CORN AND LAMB LOAVES

(6 servings)

1 pound ground lamb
1 12-ounce can whole kernel
   corn, drained

¼ teaspoon thyme
½ teaspoon salt
Pepper to taste

Combine all ingredients; mix well. Press into 6 individual loaf pans. Bake at 350° F. 45 minutes.

## MUSHROOM LAMB LOAF

(6 servings)

2 tablespoons butter or
   margarine
¼ pound mushrooms,
   chopped
1½ pounds ground lamb

1 cup finely chopped green
   pepper
1 egg, beaten
1½ cups soft bread crumbs
1 teaspoon salt
¼ teaspoon pepper

Melt butter or margarine; add mushrooms and cook until lightly browned. Combine remaining ingredients; mix well. Press half of lamb mixture into 9x5x3-inch loaf pan. Top with mushrooms. Press remaining lamb mixture over mushrooms. Bake at 350° F. 1 hour. Drain off drippings. Garnish as desired.

## POTATO-FROSTED LAMB RING

(6 servings)

2 pounds ground lamb
2 eggs, beaten
½ cup chopped green pepper
1½ cups fine dry bread crumbs
1 teaspoon salt
¼ teaspoon pepper
1 teaspoon garlic salt
3 cups seasoned mashed potatoes

Combine lamb, eggs, green pepper, crumbs, salt, pepper and garlic salt; mix well. Press into greased 8-inch ring mold. Bake at 350° F. 1 hour. Unmold. Frost with potatoes.

## LAMB CORN BREAD PIE

(4 to 6 servings)

1 pound ground lamb
1 large onion, sliced
1 teaspoon salt
⅛ teaspoon pepper
½ teaspoon lamb herbs (rosemary, dry mint leaves, grated orange rind)
1 1-pound can stewed tomatoes
1 12-ounce package corn muffin mix

Make corn muffin mix according to directions on package. Stir in parsley and celery seed. Place over meat mixture. Bake in hot oven (450°) until corn bread is golden brown and tests done. If you use a heavy iron skillet you can let the mixture stand about 10 minutes after removing from oven and it will "firm up" and turn out upside-down beautifully.

## LAMB VEGETABLE CASSEROLE I

**(4 servings)**

2½ cups diced cooked lamb
2 cups lamb gravy
1 10-ounce package frozen
    cut corn, thawed
¼ teaspoon basil

1 10-ounce package frozen
    cut green beans,
    thawed
Salt and pepper to taste

Combine lamb and gravy; mix well. Turn corn into greased 2-quart casserole; top with lamb mixture. Sprinkle with basil and top with green beans. Season with salt and pepper. Cover and bake at 350° F. 30 minutes, or until thoroughly heated.

## LAMB VEGETABLE CASSEROLE II

**(4 to 6 servings)**

2 tablespoons butter or
    margarine
1 medium-sized onion,
    chopped
1 pound lamb shoulder,
    thinly sliced

¼ teaspoon thyme
Salt and pepper to taste
3 cups seasoned mashed
    potatoes
1 10-ounce package frozen
    carrots and peas, cooked

Melt butter or margarine; add onion and cook over low heat until tender. Cut lamb into 1-inch strips. Add lamb to onion mixture and cook until lightly browned. Add thyme and salt and pepper; mix well. Spread potatoes over bottom of greased 7½x12x2-inch baking dish. Top with lamb mixture and carrots and peas. Cover and bake at 350° F. 45 minutes.

## LAMB AND VEGETABLE DINNER

(4 servings)

2 cups diced cooked lamb
1 10-ounce package frozen broccoli spears
1 1-pound can small white potatoes, drained

1 tablespoon vinegar
½ teaspoon salt
⅛ teaspoon pepper

Arrange lamb, broccoli and potatoes in greased shallow baking pan. Combine remaining ingredients; blend. Pour over lamb mixture. Cover and bake at 350° F. 30 minutes, or until broccoli is tender.

## LAMB CASSEROLE

(4 to 6 servings)

2 cups diced cooked lamb
1 10½-ounce can condensed cream of celery soup
1 4-ounce can sliced mushrooms
½ cup milk
½ teaspoon lamb herbs (rosemary, mint and grated orange peel)

Salt and pepper to taste
8 ounces shell macaroni (about 3 cups)
⅓ cup grated Parmesan cheese

## BREAST OF LAMB WITH FRUIT SAUCE

(4 servings)

3 pounds breast of lamb
1 13½-ounce can frozen
    grapefruit sections,
    thawed

1 10-ounce jar mandarin
    orange sections
2 tablespoons honey
¼ teaspoon rosemary

Place lamb on rack in roasting pan. Bake at 325° F. for 1 hour and 40 minutes. Drain off drippings. Drain grapefruit and orange sections; reserve sirups. Combine sirups, honey and rosemary; mix well. Arrange fruit sections over lamb. Pour sirup mixture over lamb. Bake 20 minutes.

## STUFFED BREAST OF LAMB

(6 to 8 servings)

1 tablespoon shortening
⅔ cup chopped onion
½ cup chopped celery
¼ cup chopped green pepper
2 tablespoons grated carrots
1 tablespoon chopped
    parsley

1 tablespoon rosemary
1 teaspoon salt
½ teaspoon pepper
4 cups soft bread crumbs
3-4 pounds boned breast of
    lamb

Melt shortening; add onions, celery and green pepper. Cook until vegetables are tender. Add carrots, parsley, rosemary, salt, pepper and bread crumbs. Put stuffing mixture on lamb; roll and tie securely. Place on rack in roasting pan and bake at 325° F. 2½ hours, or until tender.

## LAMB CURRY BAKE

(4 servings)

2 cups diced cooked lamb
1 teaspoon onion juice
½ cup sliced celery
Dash salt
Dash pepper
⅓ cup milk
1 10½-ounce can

condensed cream of
  mushroom soup
1½ cups all-purpose flour
½ teaspoon salt
2 teaspoons curry powder
½ cup shortening
3 tablespoons water

Combine lamb, onion juice, celery, dash salt, pepper, milk and soup in lightly greased 10-inch pie plate. Sift flour, ½ teaspoon salt and curry powder together. Cut in shortening. Add water; stir until well mixed. Roll out on lightly floured surface to ⅛-inch thickness. Place over lamb mixture. Seal and flute edge; slit top. Bake at 400° F. 35 minutes, or until lightly browned.


## LAMB STEAK BAKE

(4 servings)

4 lamb leg steaks, about ½
    inch thick (about 2
    pounds)
1 1½-ounce package
    dehydrated onion soup
    mix

½ cup chili sauce
1 1-pound can whole white
    potatoes, drained

Arrange lamb on rack in shallow baking pan; bake at 325° F. ½ hour. Combine soup mix and chili sauce; blend. Spread over lamb. Arrange potatoes around lamb; bake ½ hour. Baste potatoes and lamb occasionally during baking period.

Bake potatoes in hot oven (400°) 45 to 60 minutes, or until tender. Scoop out potatoes and mash. Reserve shells. Combine potatoes, butter or margarine, milk, garlic salt, pepper, lamb herbs and salt. Cook lamb until browned. Add to potato mixture; mix well. Refill potato shells. Bake at 350° F. 30 minutes.

## BAKED STUFFED PEPPERS

(4 servings—8 pepper cups)

| | |
|---|---|
| 4 large green peppers | 1 can (10½ ounces) |
| 1 small onion, chopped | condensed tomato soup |
| 1 cup cooked rice | ½ teaspoon salt |
| 1 cup shredded | ⅛ teaspoon pepper |
| quick-melting cheese | ½ teaspoon thyme |
| 2 cups finely chopped or | |
| ground left-over roast | |
| lamb | |

Cut the peppers in half lengthwise to make 8 shells. Remove cores and seeds. Boil the pepper shells in salted water for 3 minutes. Drain. Arrange them in a baking pan. Combine all remaining ingredients and spoon the mixture into the pepper shells. Bake at 350° F. for 45 minutes.

*Note:* These can be filled early, refrigerated, then put in the oven an hour before dinner.

## BAKED STUFFED TOMATOES

(3 servings)

½ pound ground lamb
6 medium or 3 large
   tomatoes
½ teaspoon salt
⅛ teaspoon pepper
⅛ teaspoon garlic salt
1 small onion, chopped

1 tablespoon prepared
   mustard
½ cup bread crumbs
1 tablespoon chopped
   parsley
½ cup catchup

Panfry the ground lamb in a skillet until all pink color disappears. Drain off excess fat. Cut tops off tomatoes. Hollow out the pulp with a spoon. Chop the pulp and add to the meat in the skillet. Add all remaining ingredients and stir to combine. Spoon stuffing into the tomato shells. (Cover top with buttered bread crumbs or shredded cheese, if desired.) Bake at 350° F. for 45 minutes.

## FRENCH BASQUE LAMB-STUFFED TOMATOES WITH BERCY SAUCE

1 cup ground cooked lamb
1 cup seasoned creamed
   mushrooms

4 medium-sized tomatoes
1 tablespoon Parmesan cheese
2 tablespoons melted butter

Hollow out tomatoes, salt inside and turn upside down to drain. Combine ground cooked lamb with 1 cup creamed mushrooms (made by creaming ¼ to ½ cup chopped canned mushrooms with 2 tablespoons butter, 2 tablespoons flour and 1 cup milk to obtain medium thick sauce). Stuff tomatoes with lamb mixture and sprinkle with Parmesan cheese and melted butter. Bake until tomato is cooked and

flake crumbs, then in undiluted evaporated milk, then again
in crumbs. Allow to stand a few minutes. Or shape in the
morning and refrigerate until ready to use. Place on a shallow pan and bake for 45 minutes at 350° F. Serve very hot,
with sauce made of condensed tomato or cream of mushroom soup.


## LAMB CHEESE ROLL

**(6 servings)**

1½  pounds ground lamb          ½  teaspoon salt
        shoulder                       ¼  teaspoon pepper
    2  eggs, slightly beaten        1  5-ounce jar processed
    1  teaspoon dry mustard             Cheddar cheese spread

Combine lamb, eggs, mustard, salt and pepper; blend. Roll
out into rectangle 14x10 inches. Dot with cheese. Roll up
jelly-roll fashion. Place seam side down on rack in shallow
roasting pan. Bake at 350° F. 45 minutes or until done.
Serve with mushroom or tomato sauce, as desired.

# SALADS

*What to do with left-over roast leg of lamb is often a question. Here are some summer and winter ideas for lamb salads that are hearty and satisfying. These make excellent luncheon entrees for family and guests. Don't hesitate to substitute lamb for any meat called for in your favorite meat salad.*

▀▄▀▄▀▄▀▄▀▄▀▄▀▄▀▄▀▄▀▄▀▄▀▄▀▄▀▄▀▄▀▄▀▄▀▄▀▄▀▄▀▄

## LAMB-STUFFED TOMATOES

**(4 servings)**

| | |
|---|---|
| 4 medium-sized tomatoes | ½ teaspoon salt |
| 4 slices cooked leg of lamb | ⅛ teaspoon pepper |
| (3x2¾x⅛-inch) | ¼ teaspoon basil |
| 2 tablespoons commercial | 32 unpared slices cucumber, |
| salad dressing | ⅛ inch thick |

Cut a slice from top of tomatoes. Scoop out pulp. Dice lamb. Combine tomato pulp, lamb, salad dressing, salt, pepper and basil; mix well. Fill tomato shells with lamb mixture. Garnish with cucumber slices. Chill 2 hours.

Combine cabbage, celery and pimientos; toss lightly and chill. Heat oil; add onion and lamb and cook until onion is tender, stirring occasionally. Add remaining ingredients; heat to boiling point. Pour lamb mixture over cabbage mixture; toss lightly but thoroughly.

## LAMB, CABBAGE AND CARROT SLAW

**(4 servings)**

2 cups diced cooked lamb
4 cups shredded cabbage
2 medium-sized carrots, grated

⅔ cup mayonnaise
½ teaspoon salt
⅛ teaspoon pepper

Combine lamb, cabbage and carrots; toss lightly. Chill. Add remaining ingredients; toss lightly but thoroughly.

## LAMB SUPPER SALAD BOWL

**(6 servings)**

4 cups diced roast lamb
½ cup coarsely chopped celery
¼ cup chopped green pepper
¼ cup sweet pickle relish
1 red-skinned apple, cut in small pieces
½ cup French dressing

1 teaspoon celery seeds
Salt, garlic salt, onion salt
Coarse-ground black pepper
Crisp lettuce or other salad greens
1 cup garlic croutons

Combine all ingredients except croutons and salad greens. Chill. Serve in salad bowl lined with crisp salad greens with croutons sprinkled over top. *Variations:* Add 1 cup cold cooked rice, omitting croutons. Or omit apple and croutons and use as filling for hollowed-out chilled tomatoes. Serve with mayonnaise.

## LAMB PLATTER WITH MINT SAUCE

(4 to 6 servings)

| | |
|---|---|
| ¼ cup chopped mint | ½ teaspoon salt |
| ¼ cup vinegar | ⅛ teaspoon pepper |
| ¼ cup sugar | 12 slices cooked lamb |
| ¼ cup water | Sliced tomatoes |

Combine mint, vinegar, sugar, water, salt and pepper; mix well. Chill. Arrange lamb and tomatoes on platter. Serve with mint sauce. Garnish as desired.

## JELLIED LAMB LOAF SALAD

(2 loaves—10 servings each)

| | |
|---|---|
| 1 square cut lamb shoulder (5½ to 6½ pounds) | 5 hard-cooked eggs |
| 5 cups cold water | ⅓ cup chopped sweet pickle |
| 1⅓ tablespoons salt | ½ cup chopped ripe olives |
| 4 whole cloves | 1½ tablespoons vinegar |
| 4 whole black peppers | 4 envelopes (4 table- |
| ½ teaspoon thyme | spoons) unflavored |
| 5 sprigs celery leaves | gelatin |

Simmer meat in water with salt, cloves, pepper, thyme, and celery leaves in a covered kettle about 2½ hours, or until very tender. Remove meat from broth and cool slightly. Strain broth through several layers of cheesecloth. Chill

## PICNIC LAMB-STUFFED TOMATOES

(6 servings)

6 medium-sized tomatoes
3 cups finely chopped cooked
    lamb
½ cup chopped celery
1 medium-sized cucumber,
    pared and chopped

⅓ cup chopped pimiento-
    stuffed green olives
½ cup mayonnaise
Salt and pepper to taste

Cut slice from tops of tomatoes. Scoop out pulp; reserve shells. Drain pulp. Combine tomato pulp, lamb, celery, cucumber, olives, mayonnaise and salt and pepper; mix well. Fill tomatoes with half of mixture. Wrap in aluminum foil. Chill. Place remaining lamb mixture in waxed container. Chill. Use as sandwich spread.

## SUMMER MOLDED LAMB SALAD

(6 to 8 servings)

2 3-ounce packages lemon-
    flavored gelatin
3½ cups hot water
1½ cups fine-chopped cooked
    lamb
½ cup chopped green
    pepper
3 tablespoons chopped
    onion
1 canned pimiento,
    chopped

1 cup chopped apple (1
    medium-sized apple)
¼ cup mayonnaise
½ cup French dressing
¼ teaspoon basil
¼ teaspoon celery salt
¼ cup chopped pimiento-
    stuffed green olives

Dissolve gelatin in water. Chill until slightly thickened. Fold in lamb, green pepper, onion, pimiento and apple. Turn into 1½-quart mold. Chill until firm. Unmold. Combine remaining ingredients; mix well. Serve olive dressing with molded lamb salad.

## LAMB MIXED VEGETABLE SALAD

(4 servings)

2 cups diced cooked lamb
1 1-pound can potatoes,
   drained and diced
1 1-pound can mixed
   vegetables, drained

¼ cup vinegar
⅓ cup French dressing
1 teaspoon celery salt
Salt and pepper to taste
Crisp salad greens

Combine lamb, potatoes and vegetables. Chill thoroughly. Combine vinegar, French dressing, celery salt and salt and pepper; blend. Add to lamb mixture; toss lightly but thoroughly. Serve on greens.

## LAMB VEGETABLE SALAD

(4 to 6 servings)

2 cups diced cooked lamb
2 medium-sized tomatoes,
   cut in wedges
1 medium-sized cucumber,
   pared and sliced

2 cups torn chicory
1 cup grated carrot
Salt and pepper to taste
½ cup French dressing

Combine lamb, tomatoes, cucumber, chicory, carrot and salt and pepper. Toss lightly. Chill thoroughly. Add dressing. Toss lightly but thoroughly.

# PATIO FARE

*There is no better meat in the world for barbecuing than lamb! Chops and steaks aren't the only lamb cuts to use for this purpose either. You'll want to try riblets, neck slices, breasts, spareribs, ground lamburger and roasts, especially a rolled shoulder roast (if you have a spit). Whether you prepare the lamb indoors or out, don't hesitate to try lamb in any favorite barbecue recipe you have, as well as those which follow. You'll find that lamb is versatile and ideal for any patio meal.*

## Lamb Steaks

If your meat dealer doesn't display lamb steaks as such, buy a "long" leg of lamb. From the sirloin end, have him cut three good slices. These sirloin steaks are sometimes called sirloin chops. Your butcher will know how to continue slicing from there until the shank end is reached. From a large leg you should have four or five good-sized steaks about an inch thick. Have the shank end boned for stew or ground for lamburgers.

Combine all ingredients in heavy saucepan. Bring to boiling point. Reduce heat. Simmer, uncovered, about 30 minutes. Serve hot over shish kebab, or other lamb dishes. With this method the onions are slightly crunchy. If desired, the onions may be cooked slowly in 3 tablespoons of butter until tender, then the remainder of ingredients added.

*Note:* Since this sauce keeps well, it may be made ahead, placed in jars, and kept in the refrigerator until ready to heat.

## GRILLED LAMB STEAKS

Keep charcoal glowing in a bed four to six inches deep. For steaks and chops about one inch thick, allow about eight minutes to each side. Use tongs for turning. To determine when the lamb steaks are cooked to your liking, use a small sharp knife and make a slit alongside the bone. Don't overcook. The meat should be juicy and still slightly pink inside for finest flavor. Season and serve on hot plates, with or without Lemon Butter below. For notes on marinades, also see "Broiler Treats" section.

## LEMON BUTTER (GOOD ON GRILLED LAMB STEAKS)

(8 servings)

| | |
|---|---|
| ½ cup butter | 2 tablespoons snipped |
| ½ teaspoon salt | parsley |
| Dash or three of Tabasco sauce | 2 tablespoons lemon juice |

Let butter stand in bowl until softened. Work with fork or wooden spoon until creamy. Add salt, Tabasco sauce, parsley. Then slowly add the lemon juice, stirring until well blended. Serve a dollop on each lamb steak. Or make in advance; using waxed paper, shape in a roll. Chill, then roll in minced parsley. Chill again. To serve, slice the chilled roll, allowing a thick slice for each serving.

*Note:* For additional ideas, see recipe for Herb Butter in "Broiler Treats" section.

## SIRLOIN STEAKS

Prepare same as round-bone leg steaks. They may cook in just slightly less time than round-bone leg steaks.

## BARBECUED LAMB RIBS

Lamb breast is a flat piece of meat 1 to 2 inches thick, with streaks of lean and fat, containing rib bones. It weighs about 2 pounds. Allow ¾ to 1 pound of lamb breast to a person. If pieces are to be left whole, have your meat dealer trim for easy carving between ribs. Or ask him to cut them into 2- or 3-rib portions, or to prepare riblets by cutting between each rib. This gives 1-inch-thick strips of lean streaked with fat, attached to a rib bone. Riblets are usually 5 to 6 inches long, weighing 2 to 4 ounces each. Lamb ribs have a delicate flavor that should be accented with subtle seasoning rather than subdued with heavy sauces, whether used for marinating or basting. There are many varieties of marinades. Most "rib" experts like to have the lamb stand in one of these sauces several hours or overnight, under refrigeration, and to use the same sauce for brushing on the lamb as it cooks. Because of the fat content of these rib portions of all meats, lamb breast (or ribs) should be cooked very slowly over sert slivers of garlic in slits at various spots around the roast. Mix together the sugar, cloves, ginger and lemon juice, and rub thoroughly into surface and ends of roast. Sprinkle with salt and pepper. Run the spit through the exact center of the rolled lamb roast. Place in the roast a short roast meat thermometer, specially designed for rotisserie use. (Remember, roasts can also be marinated in a favorite sauce a few hours or overnight, if you prefer.) Arrange spitted lamb on rotisserie, at distance above glowing coals as suggested in manufacturer's directions. Start motor for revolving spit. It is well to allow about 25 to 30 minutes per pound for meat just taken from the refrigerator, but the best guide is the use of the roast meat thermometer. The accepted internal temperature for well-done roast lamb shoulder is 180° to 182° F., but stop the cooking process at 170° to 175° F. for medium-done. The lamb will have a delicate pink tinge on the inside and will be tender and juicy. While the lamb is cooking, it may be brushed with a favorite barbecue sauce with a red or white wine and salad oil base, or with lemon juice and oil, plus seasonings of your choice, preferably without the usual tomato sauce or catchup addition. Most motored revolving spits are timed in speed so that they are self-basting, though a drip pan is often provided to catch any errant drippings. Or, a pan may be shaped of aluminum foil and placed under the spit. This prevents flare-ups of burning fat.

## BARBECUED LEG OF LAMB

Bone-in, or boneless, leg makes an excellent spitted roast. The leg with the bone in is more difficult to balance on the spit, but there are weight "balances" which may be purchased and used to compensate for the uneven pull of oddly shaped cuts of meat. A carefully balanced roast will turn evenly on the spit and not tax the motor.

The leg may be slashed in several places and shreds of peeled garlic inserted, if desired.

Legs may be marinated before roasting on the spit, or may be basted toward the end of the cooking period with a good barbecue sauce. Remember to use a meat thermometer and cook to 140°–150° for rare lamb, 170° for medium and 180°–182° for well done.

## LAMB MARINADE (FOR LEG OF LAMB)

½ cup olive or salad oil
1 cup dry red wine *or*
¼ cup lemon juice and ¾ cup pineapple juice
Snipped leaves of 2 or 3 sprigs of rosemary, thyme, marjoram, savory or oregano *or*
⅛ teaspoon powdered herbs

2 tablespoons each snipped parsley and chives
¼ teaspoon coarse-ground black pepper
½ teaspoon Worcestershire sauce
2 cloves garlic mashed with 1 teaspoon salt

*Note:* Turn the lamb occasionally, or let the marinade run to one end of the dish and spoon it over the lamb.

## BARBECUED LAMB PATTIES

(6 servings)

1½ pounds ground lamb
½ cup chopped parsley
½ cup chopped onion
¼ cup prepared mustard
¼ cup catchup

¼ cup chili sauce
2 tablespoons vinegar
½ teaspoon garlic salt
1 teaspoon sugar

Sprinkle lamb butterfly neck chops with salt and pepper. Broil them 3 or 4 inches from source of heat 5 minutes; turn, and broil about 5 minutes. Combine the catchup, sour cream and onion salt; mix well. Spread half of catchup mixture over lamb. Broil 2 minutes. Heat remaining catchup mixture to serving temperature, stirring frequently. Serve with lamb.

## LAMB KIDNEYS EN BROCHETTE

| | |
|---|---|
| 2 lamb kidneys per serving | 3 mushrooms per serving |
| 1 slice bacon per serving | Salt and pepper |

Wash kidneys in cold water. Remove outer membrane. Split in half. Remove white veins and fat with sharp-pointed knife or pair of manicure scissors. Kidneys may be cooked in milk, cold water with a little lemon juice added, or in French dressing. When tender, cut kidneys in quarters. Attach a slice of bacon to a skewer, then a piece of kidney, mushroom and the bacon again. Continue in this fashion, with the bacon running ribbon fashion on the skewer, until all ingredients are on individual skewers. Broil 3 inches from heat source about 7 minutes. Turn and broil 5 to 7 minutes more. Sprinkle with salt and pepper. Serve very hot.

## ITALIAN LAMB KEBABS

(4 servings)

| | |
|---|---|
| 2 cups 1-inch cubes lamb shoulder | Salt and pepper |
| | ¼ cup vinegar |
| 1 cup diced canned Italian red peppers | ¼ cup olive or salad oil |
| | ½ teaspoon rosemary |
| 4 slices Spanish onion | |

Arrange lamb, peppers and onion slices on skewers. Sprinkle with salt and pepper. Combine remaining ingredients;

blend. Brush kebabs with vinegar mixture. Broil 3 to 4 inches from source of heat, or cook on outdoor grill, 15 to 20 minutes, or until lamb is desired degree of doneness. Turn kebabs frequently and brush with vinegar mixture during cooking period.

## PEACH LAMB KEBABS

(4 servings)

1 pound 1-inch cubes shoulder of lamb
1 1-pound can potatoes, drained
12 dried peaches, cooked
3 tablespoons melted butter or margarine

1 tablespoon chopped parsley
¼ teaspoon dry mustard
1 teaspoon salt
¼ teaspoon pepper
Dash garlic salt
Dash onion salt

Arrange lamb, potatoes and peaches on skewers. Combine remaining ingredients; mix well. Brush kebabs with butter or margarine mixture. Broil 3 to 4 inches from source of heat, or cook on outdoor grill 15 to 20 minutes, or until lamb is desired degree of doneness. Turn kebabs and brush with butter or margarine mixture frequently during cooking period.

## GRILLED LAMB KEBABS

(6 servings)

3 cups diced lamb shoulder cubes 1½ inch square
1 medium-sized eggplant, diced
1 medium-sized green pepper, sliced into squares

12 small onions, cooked
12 small mushrooms
¼ cup butter or margarine, melted
Salt and pepper to taste

## RIB LAMB CHOPS WITH HORSE-RADISH SAUCE

(4 servings)

8 rib lamb chops, about 1 inch thick
1 cup commercial sour cream
3 tablespoons prepared horse-radish

½ teaspoon rosemary
1 teaspoon salt
¼ teaspoon pepper
½ teaspoon paprika

Broil chops 3 to 4 inches from source of heat 8 to 10 minutes. Turn and broil 6 to 8 minutes, or to desired degree of doneness. Combine remaining ingredients; mix well. Serve with chops.

## FRENCH LAMB CHOP BROIL

(4 servings)

4 French rib lamb chops
4 medium-sized potatoes, cooked
2 medium-sized tomatoes, cut in half

¼ cup melted butter or margarine
1 clove garlic, finely chopped
½ teaspoon salt
Dash pepper
¼ cup chopped parsley

Broil chops 3 to 4 inches from source of heat, about 10 minutes; turn chops. Place potatoes and tomatoes around lamb. Combine butter or margarine, garlic, salt and pepper. Pour over chops and vegetables. Broil 5 minutes or until lamb is desired degree of doneness. Sprinkle with chopped parsley.

## PARMESAN BROILED LAMB CHOPS

(4 servings)

4 rib lamb chops, about ¾ inch thick

¼ cup grated Parmesan cheese

2 tablespoons butter or margarine, softened

½ teaspoon salt

⅛ teaspoon pepper

Broil chops 3 to 4 inches from source of heat 10 to 15 minutes, or until lightly browned. Turn; broil 5 minutes or to desired degree of doneness. Combine remaining ingredients; blend. Spread on chops. Broil 2 to 3 minutes, or until cheese is lightly browned.

## SIRLOIN LAMB STEAKS WITH ORIENTAL SAUCE

(4 servings)

4 sirloin lamb steaks, about ¾ inch thick

1 9-ounce can pineapple tidbits

½ teaspoon cornstarch

¼ teaspoon soy sauce

⅓ cup flaked coconut

Broil lamb steaks 3 to 4 inches from source of heat 5 to 7 minutes. Drain pineapple; reserve sirup. Combine sirup, cornstarch and soy sauce; blend. Turn steaks; broil 4 to 5 minutes, or to desired degree of doneness. Add pineapple and coconut to sirup mixture; heat to serving temperature. Serve sauce with lamb.

## CANDIED FRUIT-GLAZED SIRLOIN STEAKS

(4 servings)

4 sirloin lamb steaks, about ¾ inch thick
½ cup water
½ cup firmly packed brown sugar
½ cup candied orange peel
½ cup seedless raisins
½ teaspoon salt
⅛ teaspoon pepper

Broil steaks 3 to 4 inches from source of heat 8 to 10 minutes, or until browned on both sides and desired degree of doneness. Meanwhile, combine remaining ingredients. Cook over low heat 5 minutes, stirring occasionally. Serve over steaks.

## MINT-GLAZED LAMB SIRLOIN STEAKS

(4 servings)

4 sirloin lamb steaks
¼ cup mint jelly
Salt and pepper
2 tablespoons chopped parsley

Broil lamb steaks 3 to 4 inches from source of heat 6 to 7 minutes, or until lightly browned. Turn. Spread with jelly; sprinkle with remaining ingredients. Broil about 5 minutes, or to desired degree of doneness.

## LAMB STEAK BROILER MEAL I

(4 to 6 servings)

2 10-ounce packages frozen peas, thawed
1 tablespoon chopped mint
2 tablespoons melted butter or margarine
½ teaspoon onion salt
2 lamb leg steaks, about ½ inch thick (about 2 pounds)
2-3 medium-sized tomatoes, cut in half

Combine peas and mint; mix lightly and turn into broiler pan. Combine butter or margarine and onion salt; blend. Place broiler rack over pea mixture. Arrange lamb steaks on rack. Broil 3 to 4 inches from source of heat 10 minutes. Turn steaks. Arrange tomatoes on rack. Broil 10 minutes, or until lamb is desired degree of doneness. Brush tomatoes with onion salt mixture frequently during broiling period.

## LAMB STEAK BROILER MEAL II

(4 servings)

1 teaspoon paprika
1 teaspoon salt
½ teaspoon thyme
½ teaspoon marjoram
1 clove garlic, finely chopped
½ cup vinegar
¼ cup salad oil

4 medium-sized potatoes, cut into ½-inch strips
2 lamb leg steaks, about ½ inch thick (about 2 pounds)
2 medium-sized tomatoes, cut in half crosswise

Combine paprika, salt, thyme, marjoram, garlic, vinegar and oil; mix well. Add potatoes and lamb. Chill 1 hour. Drain lamb and potatoes; reserve ½ cup dressing. Arrange potatoes on broiler rack. Broil 3 to 4 inches from source of heat 20 minutes, or until almost tender. Turn occasionally during broiling period. Arrange lamb and tomatoes on broiler rack with potatoes; brush with dressing. Broil 10 minutes. Turn lamb and potatoes; brush with remaining dressing mixture. Broil 5 minutes, or until lamb is desired degree of doneness.

## LAMB STEAKS WITH GOLDEN SAUCE

(4 servings)

2 lamb leg steaks, about ½       ½ teaspoon salt
   inch thick                     ⅛ teaspoon pepper
2 tablespoons butter or          ½ cup milk
   margarine                       ½ cup chicken bouillon
1 medium-sized onion, sliced     1 hard-cooked egg
2 tablespoons all-purpose        Paprika
   flour

Broil lamb steaks 3 to 4 inches from source of heat 10 to 12 minutes, or until lightly browned on both sides. Meanwhile, melt butter or margarine; add onion and cook until tender. Add flour, salt and pepper and blend. Gradually add milk and bouillon and cook over low heat, stirring constantly, until thickened. Remove egg yolk from egg white; chop white. Sieve yolk. Add egg white to cream sauce. Heat to serving temperature, stirring occasionally. Sprinkle with egg yolk and paprika. Serve with lamb steaks.

## LAMB STEAK AND VEGETABLE DINNER

(4 servings)

2 12-ounce cans whole kernel     2 lamb leg steaks, about ¾
   corn                               inch thick
¼ pound mushrooms, sliced        1 8-ounce can tomato sauce
   Salt, pepper and garlic salt    ½ cup grated Cheddar cheese

Arrange corn and mushrooms in broiler pan. Sprinkle with salt, pepper and garlic salt. Place lamb steaks on broiler rack, over corn mixture. Sprinkle with salt, pepper and garlic salt. Broil 3 to 4 inches from source of heat 10 minutes. Turn lamb steaks. Broil to desired degree of doneness. Combine tomato sauce and cheese. Heat to serving temperature. Serve over lamb steaks.

## LAMB STEAKS WITH MUSHROOM-PIMIENTO SAUCE

(4 servings)

2 lamb leg steaks, about ½ inch thick
2 tablespoons butter or margarine
½ cup sliced mushrooms
2 tablespoons all-purpose flour
2 teaspoons prepared horse-radish
½ teaspoon salt
⅛ teaspoon pepper
1 cup milk
2 tablespoons diced canned pimiento

Broil lamb steaks 3 to 4 inches from source of heat 10 to 12 minutes, or until lightly browned on both sides. Meanwhile, melt butter or margarine; add mushrooms and cook 5 minutes. Add flour, horse-radish, salt and pepper and blend. Gradually add milk and cook over low heat, stirring constantly, until thickened. Add pimiento and mix well. Serve with lamb steaks.

## MINT-GLAZED LAMB STEAKS

(4 servings)

4 lamb leg steaks, about ½ inch thick (about 2 pounds)
½ cup mint jelly
Salt and pepper
¼ cup chopped parsley

Broil lamb steaks 3 to 4 inches from source of heat 6 to 7 minutes, or until lightly browned. Turn. Spread with jelly;

sprinkle with remaining ingredients. Broil 5 minutes, or to
desired degree of doneness.

## LAMB SHOULDER CHOPS WITH MINT SAUCE

(4 servings)

4 lamb shoulder chops, about     ¼ cup water
    ¾ inch thick                     ¼ cup mint jelly
Salt and pepper

Sprinkle chops with salt and pepper. Place on broiler rack
and broil 3 to 4 inches from source of heat 10 to 12 minutes,
or to desired degree of doneness. Turn chops during broiling period. Drain off drippings from broiler pan. Reserve 2
tablespoons drippings. Add water to 2 tablespoons drippings; heat to boiling point. Add jelly; mix well. Cook until
jelly is melted, stirring frequently. Serve with chops.

## BROILED LAMB SHOULDER CHOPS
## WITH STUFFED PEACHES

(4 servings)

4 shoulder lamb chops          ¼ cup currant jelly
  Salt and pepper to taste     2 tablespoons chopped
2 tablespoons butter or            almonds
   margarine                   4 canned peach halves, well
2 tablespoons chopped              drained
   parsley

Sprinkle lamb with salt and pepper. Combine butter or margarine and parsley. Brush lamb with parsley mixture. Broil
3 to 4 inches from source of heat 5 to 7 minutes. Combine

currant jelly and almonds; mix well. Fill center of peach halves with jelly mixture. Turn lamb; brush with remaining parsley mixture. Arrange peach halves around chops. Broil 4 to 5 minutes, or until lamb is desired degree of doneness.

## BROILED LAMB SHOULDER CHOPS WITH TOMATO TOPPING

(4 servings)

2 tablespoons tomato paste  
¼ cup chopped onion  
1 tablespoon vinegar  
1 tablespoon salad oil  
½ teaspoon oregano  
½ teaspoon salt  
4 lamb shoulder chops, about  
    ¾ inch thick

Combine tomato paste, onion, vinegar, oil, oregano and salt; mix well. Broil lamb chops 3 to 4 inches from source of heat 8 minutes. Turn; spread with tomato paste mixture. Broil 7 minutes, or to desired degree of doneness.

## PINEAPPLE LAMB PATTIES

(4 servings)

1 1-pound 13-ounce can  
    sliced pineapple  
3 slices bread  
1½ pounds ground lamb  
1 egg, beaten  
½ cup chopped onion  
1 teaspoon salt  
¼ teaspoon pepper  
½ teaspoon rosemary

Drain pineapple; reserve ⅔ cup sirup. Soak bread in ⅔ cup sirup. Add remaining ingredients. Mix well. Shape into 8 patties. Broil 3 to 4 inches from source of heat 6 to 8 minutes. Turn and top with pineapple slices. Broil 6 minutes. If desired, top center of each patty with a stuffed olive or a cooked prune.

## BLUE CHEESE-TOPPED PATTIES

(See Lamburger Variations in Sandwich section.)

## LAMB VEGETABLE BURGERS

(6 servings)

1½ pounds ground lamb
    shoulder
1 medium-sized onion,
    chopped
1 small green pepper,
    chopped

1 canned pimiento,
    chopped
2 eggs, slightly beaten
2 cups finely diced cooked
    potatoes
2 teaspoons salt

Combine all ingredients; mix well. Shape into 12 patties, about ½ inch thick. Broil 3 to 4 inches from source of heat 5 minutes. Turn; broil 5 minutes, or to desired degree of doneness. Serve with tomato sauce, as desired.

## PICKLE LAMBURGERS

(4 servings)

1 pound ground lamb shoulder
2 tablespoons onion, chopped
1 cup sweet mixed pickles,
    chopped

1 tablespoon prepared
    mustard
Salt and pepper to taste

Combine all ingredients. Shape into 4 patties, about 1 inch thick. Broil 3 to 4 inches from source of heat 5 minutes. Turn and broil 5 minutes, or to desired degree of doneness.

## HOW TO MAKE LAMB CHOPLETS or "Scotch Chops" at Home (Available ready-made in many markets)

Buy a supply of inch-thick riblets at the market, allowing two to a person. At the same time, buy a quantity of freshly ground lamb. With a sharp knife, make a slash along the bone, starting just above one end of the bone and extending about two-thirds the length of the riblet. Pry open and stuff ground lamb into this slash, patting it flat to resemble a rib chop. Store between strips of wax paper in the refrigerator until ready to broil.

Place on broiler rack about 3 inches from source of heat. Broil top, sprinkle with salt and pepper, a dash of thyme or garlic, if desired. Turn with tongs or turner and continue to broil until done. Serve for Sunday brunch, lunch or dinner.

*Note:* This sauce is excellent on choplets: Melt over low heat one cup currant or mint jelly, whipping until smooth. If using currant jelly, stir in one teaspoon prepared mustard. Serve hot over choplets.

## LAMB ASPARAGUS ROLLS

(4 servings)

1 8-ounce can tomato sauce
1 tablespoon butter or
    margarine
¼ cup finely chopped onion
½ teaspoon garlic salt

¼ teaspoon salt
1 14½-ounce can asparagus
    spears, drained
4 slices cooked lamb

Add lamb and heat to serving temperature, stirring occasionally. Serve on toast.

## CRANBERRY NECK SLICES

(4 servings)

4 ¾-inch lamb neck slices (about 1¼ pounds)
Seasoned flour
1 tablespoon salad oil
1 clove garlic, finely chopped
½ cup water
¼ cup pineapple juice
1 cup canned cranberries
2 tablespoons sugar
1 teaspoon salt
¼ teaspoon pepper
1 teaspoon Worcestershire sauce

Coat lamb with flour. Heat oil; add lamb and garlic. Cook until lamb is lightly browned on both sides. Combine remaining ingredients. Add to lamb mixture. Cover and cook over low heat 45 minutes, or until lamb is tender.

## LAMB TERRAPIN

(4 servings)

2 tablespoons butter
2 tablespoons flour
1 teaspoon dry mustard
1 cup stock from lamb bones, or chicken broth, or milk
2½ cups diced cold lamb from roast
3 hard-cooked eggs, chopped
3 tablespoons olive oil
1 teaspoon Worcestershire sauce
Pinch of thyme, marjoram, or both
Salt and pepper

Melt butter in frying pan. Stir in flour and dry mustard; mix well. Add stock from lamb bones, or chicken broth, or milk, stirring constantly. When thickened, add diced cold lamb from roast, and hard-cooked eggs, chopped, mixed together with olive oil. Season with Worcestershire sauce, thyme and/or marjoram, and salt and pepper. Cover and simmer 5 minutes or heat over hot water in double boiler. Serve on hot buttered toast. Sherry to taste may be used instead of seasonings.

## LAMB BREAKFAST SAUSAGE

(6 to 7 servings)

1 pound lean ground lamb
⅓ pound ground pork
⅛ teaspoon coarse-ground
    pepper
½ teaspoon salt

¼ teaspoon powdered
    marjoram
¼ teaspoon powdered
    thyme
¼-½ teaspoon powdered sage

If dried herbs are used, crush to a powder between the fingers or with handle of ice pick in a shallow wooden bowl. Poultry seasoning or all sage may be used. Lamb alone may be used but the pork may be added, if desired. Mix all ingredients together thoroughly. Cover bowl with waxed paper, foil, or bowl cover. Place in refrigerator overnight if possible. To use, shape into patties of desired size, about ½ inch thick. Cook over moderate heat in heavy skillet until brown. Turn. Brown other side. Lower heat to cook through. (If you use the pork it should be well-done.) Serve piping hot. Good breakfast mates for a leisurely Sunday meal are lamb sausage patties and country gravy (the drippings make such good cream gravy), butter-browned pineapple slices or

Cook onion slowly in melted butter in heavy frying pan until tender but not brown. Pull to one side of pan. Add lamb. Cook until browned, pulling apart with a fork or pancake turner. Stir in flour and seasonings. Cook a few minutes, then add bouillon and simmer about 15 minutes. Remove from heat. Stir in sour cream. Both filling and pancakes may be made ahead and placed in refrigerator until cool. Then roll the filling in the pancakes and place in heatproof shallow dish. Or put together for heating in oven just before serving. Just before serving, place a good-sized spoonful of the lamb filling in middle of each pancake. Pull pancake edges up over filling, overlap. Hold in place with a toothpick. Place filled pancakes in shallow baking dish or heatproof platter. To bake: Drizzle a little melted butter over pancakes. Sprinkle with grated Parmesan cheese. Bake in a 400° F. (hot) oven, about 8 minutes.

Serve piping hot with a choice of toppings—sour cream, Parmesan cheese, or a cranberry relish.

## LAMB SHOULDER CHOPS WITH CAPER SAUCE

**(4 servings)**

| | |
|---|---|
| 2 tablespoons butter or margarine | ¼ cup butter or margarine |
| 4 shoulder lamb chops, about ½ inch thick | ¼ cup mayonnaise |
| Salt and pepper | 1 tablespoon prepared mustard |
| | 1 tablespoon capers |

Melt 2 tablespoons butter or margarine in large skillet; add chops. Sprinkle with salt and pepper. Cook until lightly browned on both sides. Cover and cook 20 minutes, or until tender. Combine remaining ingredients and cook over low heat 10 minutes, stirring frequently.

## SOUR CREAM LAMB STEW

(4 servings)

2 tablespoons butter or margarine
1½ pounds cubed lamb shoulder
3 medium-sized onions, sliced
1 medium-sized green pepper, sliced

1½ teaspoons salt
2 teaspoons paprika
1 cup water
1 cup commercial sour cream

Melt butter or margarine. Add lamb and cook until browned on all sides. Add onions, green pepper, salt and paprika. Cover; cook over low heat 15 minutes. Add water. Cover and cook 1 to 1½ hours, or until lamb is tender. Add sour cream; mix well. Heat to serving temperature over low heat.

## DELICIOUS LAMB MEAT BALLS

(6 servings)

1½ pounds ground lamb
1 cup soft bread cubes
1 egg, slightly beaten
¼ cup milk
3 tablespoons catchup
1 teaspoon salt
Dash pepper
½ teaspoon rosemary
2 tablespoons butter or margarine

2 medium-sized onions, sliced
1 10-ounce package frozen peas
1 cup water
½ cup vinegar
2 tablespoons sugar
1 teaspoon salt
⅛ teaspoon pepper

Combine lamb, bread cubes, egg, milk, catchup, 1 teaspoon salt, dash pepper and rosemary. Mix well. Shape into 12 1½-inch balls. Melt butter or margarine. Add lamb; cook until browned on all sides. Remove lamb. Drain drippings; reserve 2 tablespoons. Cook onions in reserved drippings until lightly browned. Add peas, water, vinegar, sugar, 1 teaspoon salt and ⅛ teaspoon pepper. Mix well. Add lamb balls. Cover; cook over low heat 30 minutes, or until done.


## SAVORY LAMB SHORT RIBS

**(4 to 6 servings)**

2 pounds lamb short ribs
2 tablespoons melted butter
   or margarine
2 medium-sized onions,
   chopped
1 cup sliced celery
1 6-ounce can tomato paste

¼ cup firmly packed brown
   sugar
2 cups water
2 tablespoons vinegar
2 tablespoons all-purpose
   flour
Salt to taste

Cook short ribs in butter or margarine until browned on all sides. Add onions, celery, tomato paste, sugar and water. Cover and cook over low heat, stirring occasionally, 1 hour or until lamb is tender. Combine vinegar and flour; mix well. Gradually add to lamb mixture and cook, stirring constantly, until thickened. Season with salt.


## BRAISED LAMB RIBLETS

**(4 servings)**

2 pounds lamb riblets
1 tablespoon melted butter
   or margarine
½ cup sliced celery
2 large onions, sliced
2 cups vegetable juice
   cocktail

2 tablespoons all-purpose
   flour
1 tablespoon vinegar
Salt and onion salt to taste

Cook lamb in butter or margarine until well browned on all sides. Drain off drippings. Add celery, onions and 1¾ cups vegetable juice cocktail; cover and cook over low heat 1 hour, or until lamb is tender. Combine flour and remaining vegetable juice cocktail; blend. Gradually add flour mixture to lamb; cook over low heat, stirring constantly, until thickened. Add remaining ingredients; mix well.

## CURRANT-GLAZED LAMB PATTIES

(6 servings)

1½ pounds ground lamb
1 small onion, chopped
2 teaspoons salt
1 tablespoon capers
  (optional)

Melted butter or
  margarine
⅓ cup currant jelly

Combine lamb, onion, salt and capers; mix well. Shape into patties, about 1 inch thick. Cook in small amount of butter or margarine until browned on both sides. Add jelly and cook, covered, over low heat, to desired degree of doneness.

## SPAGHETTI AND LAMB MEAT BALLS

(4 servings)

1 pound ground lamb
  shoulder
1 egg, slightly beaten
½ teaspoon salt
¼ teaspoon pepper
2 tablespoons salad oil
¼ cup chopped onion

1 clove garlic, finely chopped
1 1-pound can tomatoes
1 8-ounce can tomato sauce
1 teaspoon oregano
  Salt and pepper to taste
8 ounces spaghetti

Combine lamb, egg, ½ teaspoon salt and ¼ teaspoon pepper; blend. Shape into 16 meat balls. Heat oil; add lamb meat balls, garlic, onion, tomatoes and tomato sauce, oregano and salt and pepper. Cover and cook over low heat 45 minutes, stirring occasionally. Meanwhile, cook spaghetti in boiling salted water in usual manner, and drain.

Serve spaghetti with lamb meat balls and sauce, accompanied by a mixed green salad.

## LAMB STEW WITH ROSEMARY

(6 servings)

¼ cup butter or margarine
1 large onion, sliced
2 cups lamb stock or chicken
   bouillon
4 cups diced cooked lamb
4 cups diced potatoes
2 cups sliced carrots

1 10-ounce package frozen
   peas
1 cup catchup
1 teaspoon salt
¼ teaspoon pepper
½ teaspoon rosemary

Melt butter or margarine; add onion and cook until lightly browned. Add remaining ingredients. Cover and cook over low heat 40 minutes, stirring occasionally.

## LAMB (GROUND) STROGANOFF— A "QUICKIE" VERSION

(6 servings)

½ cup minced onion
1 clove garlic, minced
  (optional)
1½ pounds ground lamb
1 3- or 4-ounce can sliced
   mushrooms
2 teaspoons salt

¼ teaspoon pepper
¼ teaspoon paprika
3 tablespoons flour
1 cup bouillon
1 cup commercial sour
   cream

Sauté onion and garlic slowly in 1 tablespoon fat for approximately 5 minutes, until soft and golden; stir in ground lamb, mushrooms, salt, pepper and paprika, and cook 5 minutes. Mix in flour; stir in bouillon and simmer 10 minutes, or until lamb is done. Stir in sour cream; heat, but do not boil. Serve on hot cooked rice or noodles.

## LAMB STROGANOFF I

(6 servings)

1½ pounds boneless lamb shoulder, thinly sliced
Seasoned flour
⅓ cup butter or margarine
1 clove garlic, finely chopped
½ cup chopped onion
1 pound mushrooms, sliced
Salt and pepper to taste
1½ cups sour cream
3 tablespoons dry sherry (optional)

Coat lamb with flour. Melt butter or margarine; add lamb, garlic and onions and cook until lamb is lightly browned on all sides. Add mushrooms and salt and pepper. Cover and cook over low heat 20 minutes, stirring occasionally. Add cream and sherry and mix well.
Serve with cooked rice, as desired.

## LAMB STROGANOFF II

(4 servings)

1 pound boneless lamb shoulder, thinly sliced
Seasoned flour
¼ cup butter or margarine
1 clove garlic, finely chopped
½ cup chopped onion
1 pound mushrooms, sliced
1 10½-ounce can condensed cream of celery soup
Salt and pepper to taste
1 cup sour cream

the beans in 1 quart of cold water overnight or pour the water over the beans in a covered saucepan and bring to the boiling point. Boil 2 or 3 minutes. Do not remove lid. Remove pan from heat and let stand 1 hour. After the beans are soaked, put the beans and water in a heavy kettle. Add the 1½ quarts water, salt, the bouquet garni and the lamb bones which your meat dealer will give you after boning a lamb shoulder for you. Cover tightly. Bring to the boiling point. Reduce heat to a simmer and cook slowly until the beans are tender. This may be done on the surface of the range, or for really fine flavor, in a very slow oven (225° F.) nearly all day, or until beans are completely tender.

### To prepare the meat:

2 or 2½ pounds boneless lamb, cut in 1-inch cubes

2 tablespoons butter or olive oil

1 cup coarsely chopped onion

1 clove minced garlic

1 cup tomato sauce *or*

1 cup dry white wine mixed with

3 tablespoons tomato paste

½ teaspoon salt

¼ teaspoon coarse-ground black pepper

Brown the lamb in butter or oil in a heavy frying pan or Dutch oven. Then add chopped onions and continue cooking to brown a little. Add garlic and tomato sauce or white wine and tomato paste. Cover and simmer for about 1½ hours or until the lamb is tender. It may be necessary to add a little white wine or some of the bean stock.

### To prepare the Cassoulet:

¼ pound salami or Italian sausage, skinned and cut in ½-inch cubes *or*

6 small link sausages, fried, then cut in thirds

The beans, drained

The bean stock

The lamb

Drain the beans, removing the bones and bouquet garni, reserving the liquid. Put a layer of the beans in a large casserole, then a layer of the lamb and the salami or sausages. Repeat. Pour the gravy from the lamb and enough of the bean stock to cover the beans. Cover tightly and bake in a 300° F. (slow) oven for 2 hours, adding more bean stock if mixture seems dry.

*To serve:* Ladle from casserole into bowls. Serve with chilled buttered rye bread slices, a green salad, and dry white wine, if desired. This dish can be reheated two or three times and seems to improve, so better double the recipe!

## HERBED LAMB AND CORN

(4 to 6 servings)

2 tablespoons salad oil
1½ pounds cubed boneless
    lamb shoulder
2 large onions, sliced
1 cup chopped mushrooms

1 1-pound can cream-style
    corn
1 teaspoon lamb herbs
Salt and pepper to taste

Heat oil; add lamb and onions and cook until lightly browned, stirring occasionally. Add remaining ingredients. Cover and cook over low heat 30 minutes, or until the lamb is tender, stirring occasionally.

## VEGETABLE LAMB STEW

(4 servings)

1½ pounds diced boneless
    lamb shoulder
Seasoned flour
2 tablespoons salad oil
2 cloves garlic, finely
    chopped

2 cups water
1 10-ounce package frozen
    mixed vegetables
Salt and pepper to taste
½ teaspoon rosemary

being made. Left-over stew may also be edged with fluffy mashed potatoes. Brush with butter and bake, or top with flaky pastry.

## LAMB STEW WITH CARAWAY

(4 servings)

1-1½ pounds lamb stew meat
    (or lamb shoulder cut
    for stew)
  1 tablespoon fat
    Salt, pepper, garlic salt
  2 tablespoons flour
    Water
  ¼ cup white wine, if
    desired

  1 teaspoon caraway seeds,
    if desired
  4 medium potatoes, pared
    and cut in large cubes
  8 small onions, peeled
4-6 carrots, scraped and
    sliced thick

Melt fat in skillet. Add lamb and brown well on all sides, using moderate heat. Sprinkle with salt, pepper, garlic salt, and flour, stirring well to coat lamb. Add water to not quite cover meat, and white wine if desired, or more water if liquid cooks too low. Sprinkle in caraway seeds, if used. Cover tightly and cook slowly 45 minutes. Add vegetables, sprinkle with a bit more salt and chopped parsley, if you have it. Cover and cook slowly about 30 minutes more or until lamb and vegetables are fork-tender. When meat and vegetables are cooked, the stew may be topped with dumplings to steam as recipe indicates. A bit of minced parsley may be added to the dumplings instead of the stew.

## CHILI LAMB

(4 servings)

2 tablespoons butter
1 pound boned diced lamb
½ cup chili sauce
1 teaspoon Worcestershire
    sauce

½ teaspoon salt
¼ teaspoon chili powder
Dash Tabasco sauce

Melt butter, add lamb and cook over low heat until lightly browned on all sides. Add chili sauce, Worcestershire sauce, salt, chili powder and dash Tabasco sauce; mix well. Cover and cook over low heat, stirring occasionally, one hour.

## BRAISED LAMB NECK SLICES IN SOUR CREAM

(4 servings)

2 pounds lamb neck slices
⅓ cup flour
1½ teaspoons salt
⅛ teaspoon pepper
2 tablespoons fat or oil
½ cup chopped onion
3 bouillon cubes dissolved
    in

3 cups boiling water
1 tablespoon white wine *or*
1 tablespoon lemon juice
½-1 teaspoon crushed dried
    oregano or thyme
Garlic clove on toothpick
1 cup dairy-sour cream

Mix together flour and seasonings. Coat lamb with flour mixture. (Lamb may be cut from bone if desired.) Brown well in hot fat in skillet over moderate heat. Add all ingredients except sour cream. Reduce heat to very low. Cover skillet and allow to simmer for 2 hours or until tender, adding a bit of water if it cooks low. Push lamb to one side of skillet.

Stir in sour cream. Heat slowly. Serve very hot over cooked fine noodles, sprinkling liberally with paprika and cut chives if desired. Caraway seeds, ¼ teaspoon, may be added along with the other seasonings.

## LAMB SHOULDER CHOPS WITH PINEAPPLE

(4 servings)

3 tablespoons butter or margarine

4 lamb shoulder chops, about 1 inch thick

1 1-pound 4-ounce can pineapple chunks

1 medium-sized green pepper, chopped

1 tablespoon soy sauce

Melt butter or margarine; add chops and brown on one side. Turn and add pineapple chunks, green pepper and soy sauce. Cover; cook over low heat 45 minutes, or until lamb is tender.

## LAMB CHOPS ORIENTAL

(4 servings)

4 shoulder lamb chops

1 medium-sized onion, sliced

1 large green pepper, cut in strips

¾ cup water

3 chicken bouillon cubes

½ teaspoon lamb herbs

(rosemary, dry mint leaves and grated orange rind)

1½ teaspoons salt

Pepper to taste

½ teaspoon garlic salt

1 bay leaf

1 1-pound can bean sprouts

Cook lamb over low heat until browned on both sides. Add onion and green pepper; cook 5 minutes. Add water, bouillon cubes, lamb herbs, salt, pepper, garlic salt, bay leaf and undrained bean sprouts. Cook, covered, over low heat 30 minutes. Remove bay leaf.

## SHOULDER LAMB CHOPS WITH ONIONS AND GREEN BEANS

(4 servings)

4 shoulder lamb chops, ¾ inch thick
2 cups water
2 beef bouillon cubes
1 1-pound can white onions

1 10-ounce package frozen French-style green beans
1½ teaspoons salt
½ teaspoon rosemary

Cook chops over low heat until browned on both sides. Add water and bouillon cubes. Cook, covered, over low heat 30 minutes. Add undrained onions, green beans, salt and rosemary. Cook, covered, 8 to 10 minutes, or until green beans are tender.

## LAMB AND MIXED VEGETABLE SKILLET

(6 servings)

2 tablespoons butter or margarine
2 pounds boneless lamb shoulder, diced
1 medium-sized onion, sliced
1 medium-sized green pepper, diced
¼ cup all-purpose flour

2 12-ounce cans whole kernel corn
1 1-pound 13-ounce can tomatoes
1 6-ounce can tomato paste
1 teaspoon salt
¼ teaspoon pepper

Melt butter or margarine; add lamb, onion and green pepper. Cook until lamb is lightly browned, stirring occasionally. Add flour and blend. Add remaining ingredients. Cover and cook over low heat 1 hour, or until lamb is tender, stirring occasionally.

## NEW ENGLAND BOILED LAMB DINNER

(6 servings)

1 3- to 4-pound boned lamb shoulder, rolled and tied
Water
5 whole peppercorns
2 bay leaves
1 teaspoon thyme
½ teaspoon lamb herbs (rosemary, dry mint leaves and grated orange rind)
1 tablespoon salt
6 medium-sized potatoes, pared
12 small white onions
6 medium-sized carrots, pared
1 small head cabbage, cut in wedges

Cover lamb with water. Add seasonings. Cover and cook over low heat 1½ hours. Add potatoes, onions and carrots. Cover and cook 30 minutes, or until lamb and vegetables are tender. Add cabbage. Cover and cook 10 minutes.

## LAMB RICE AND MUSHROOM SKILLET

(4 servings)

2 tablespoons butter or margarine
1 pound ground lamb
1 3-ounce can mushrooms
2 8-ounce cans tomato sauce
1 1-pound can tomatoes
1 cup uncooked rice
1 teaspoon salt
¼ teaspoon pepper
1 teaspoon Worcestershire sauce

Melt butter or margarine; add lamb and cook until lightly browned, stirring occasionally. Add remaining ingredients. Cover and cook 30 minutes or until rice is tender, stirring occasionally.

## LAMB MARBLES

(6 servings—24 meat balls, 1¼ inches in diameter)

1 pound ground lamb
2 slices bread
¼ cup minced onion
1 egg
1 teaspoon salt
¼ teaspoon pepper

¼ teaspoon thyme seasoning
    powder
1 teaspoon cornstarch
½ cup milk
Butter or drippings for
    browning

Hold bread (dry if you have it) under running water long enough to moisten it. Squeeze out excess water. Whip it with a fork. Cook onion briefly in butter. Add to bread along with lamb and other ingredients. Mix until thoroughly combined. Chill if possible. Mixture is soft. Shape mixture in balls about the size of a large walnut, easier done if the hands are wet and a teaspoon is used for rounding up a scoop of the lamb. There should be 20 to 24 meat balls. They may be made smaller, if desired. Brown in butter or drippings in skillet over moderate heat, turning balls carefully to have all sides browned evenly. Don't crowd. Remove the meat balls to a heavy saucepan as they are browned. Make desired sauce in skillet. They may be heated in the sauce or baked in a 350° F. (moderate) oven about 20 minutes or until hot.

### Burgundy Sauce:

Into fat left in skillet, stir 4 tablespoons flour. Cook over low heat for a few minutes, then pour in 1½ cups water and 1 cup Burgundy or claret wine. Add 2 bouillon cubes, salt if necessary, and cook, stirring all the time, until smooth. Pour this sauce over the lamb marbles and set aside for ½ hour before serving, then heat thoroughly on top of range or in a moderate oven.

### Consommé Sauce:

Use 1 can (10½ ounces) consommé and 1 cup water as the liquid in above recipe. Add chopped parsley just before serving, if desired.

### Sour Cream Sauce:

Add 2 tablespoons flour to the drippings left from browning the marbles. Stir in well, then add 1 cup water. Cook until thickened. Reduce heat. Stir in 1 cup dairy-sour cream, 1 tablespoon chopped parsley, ¼ teaspoon garlic salt, and 1 teaspoon paprika. Add lamb marbles and simmer about 10 minutes, or cook in a moderate oven. For an unusual flavor, stir in 2 to 3 teaspoons curry powder along with the flour, omitting the paprika.

*To prepare for the freezer:* Brown the lamb meat balls, pack in refrigerator containers and pour over them the desired sauce to within ½ inch of top. Seal according to container manufacturer's directions. Or, using foil baking dishes, place lamb balls on a bed of cooked noodles. Pour sauce over all. Seal with film.

*To use* these "casseroled" dishes, heat in moderate oven, thawing in refrigerator first, if desired.

## ORANGE-GLAZED LAMB SHOULDER CHOPS

(4 servings)

4 blade or round bone
   shoulder lamb chops
2 tablespoons butter
   Salt and pepper
2 tablespoons chopped
   parsley
½ teaspoon dry mustard

½ teaspoon garlic salt
½ cup orange juice
1 tablespoon grated orange
   rind, if desired
4 teaspoons cornstarch
1½ cups water

Heat butter in heavy frying pan or automatic electric skillet. Add chops and brown slowly on both sides. Sprinkle with salt and pepper. Remove chops to a plate. To the drippings in the skillet, add the parsley, seasonings, orange juice and grated peel, and 1 cup water. Bring to the boiling point. Add remaining water mixed with the cornstarch. Boil and stir until thick and clear. Return chops to skillet. Cover tightly and cook until fork-tender, about 45 minutes for ¾-inch-thick chops. White wine may be used in place of the orange juice or to replace ½ cup of the water.

## BRAISED LAMB SHOULDER CHOPS

(4 servings)

4 lamb shoulder chops
   Cut clove of garlic
1 tablespoon butter or
   margarine
2 tablespoons butter
2 medium-sized yellow
   onions, thinly sliced
¼ pound fresh mushrooms,
   sliced

2 tablespoons flour
1 teaspoon tomato paste
¾ cup water or chicken or
   meat stock
½ cup dry white wine or
   water or stock
   Salt
   Coarse-ground black
   pepper

Rub chops with cut clove of garlic. Put 1 tablespoon butter or shortening in a heavy skillet. When melted and hot, brown chops rather quickly on both sides. Melt the 2 table-spoons butter in a heavy saucepan or another skillet. Add onions and mushrooms and cook over medium heat until just beginning to brown. Remove from heat; blend in flour, then tomato paste. Add the water or stock and wine or stock as desired, and stir over heat until the mixture starts to boil. Add salt and pepper. Pour off any of the lamb fat that may have been cooked out of the chops. Pour sauce over chops. Cover skillet and simmer about 40 minutes or until the chops are fork-tender. Serve hot. This dish can wait almost indef-initely over a simmering heat. It is an excellent dish for your electric skillet!

## LAMB SHOULDER CHOPS, PIZZA STYLE

1 ¾-inch lamb shoulder
  chop per serving
Salt and coarse-ground
  black pepper
Garlic salt
1 tablespoon tomato paste
  per chop
⅛ teaspoon oregano

(marjoram or thyme may
  be substituted) per chop
1 slice Mozzarella cheese
  per chop
Parsley, chopped
Strips of anchovies, if
  desired

Brown each chop slowly on both sides in a small amount of butter or drippings. Sprinkle each with salt, coarse-ground black pepper, garlic salt. Spread tomato paste over each chop, then sprinkle with oregano, marjoram or thyme. Top each chop with a slice of Mozzarella cheese. Spread cheese with an additional teaspoon of tomato paste. Sprinkle lib-erally with chopped parsley and, if you like, add strips of flat-packed anchovies. Cover skillet tightly and simmer very slowly until chops are fork-tender, about 45 minutes. If moisture is needed a bit of tomato juice, stock or water may be added. Serve piping hot, with Risotto, and a tossed salad.

## RISOTTO

(6 to 8 servings)

2 cups uncooked rice
½ cup olive oil or butter
2 tablespoons minced onion
2 small cloves crushed garlic
1 quart soup stock made from
    lamb bones, or chicken
    bouillon cubes

Pinch of sweet basil or
    saffron
Mushroom pieces, browned
    in butter

Place rice in heavy skillet with olive oil or butter. Heat slowly and stir lightly, gently but constantly, with wooden spoon or fork. Presently the white rice will begin to show a yellow tinge. As it absorbs the oil or butter, add more to keep rice moist. Add the minced onion and garlic. Continue to cook rice to a deep gold color. Turn off heat. Have ready hot soup stock. Pour hot stock gradually over rice, stirring gently. When well moistened, season as desired. A pinch of sweet basil is good, or a very slight amount of saffron. Transfer the risotto to a casserole, cover, and put in a 350° F. oven for 40 to 45 minutes, removing it when rice is soft, yet still firm, with the grains separate. Lightly stir in with a fork some mushroom pieces browned in butter.

*Note:* For a meal in itself, cut ½ pound of lamb liver into small thick strips. Quickly brown all over in 2 tablespoons butter. Stir into the rice mixture before placing in casserole. A tablespoonful of tomato paste stirred into the stock gives a good flavor for this main dish risotto.

## "PORCUPINE" LAMB MEAT BALLS

### (6 servings—24 meat balls)

| | |
|---|---|
| 1 pound ground lamb | 1 can (10½ ounces) |
| ½ cup uncooked rice | consommé |
| ⅔ cup finely chopped onion | ½ cup catchup |
| 1 teaspoon salt | ½ teaspoon sweet basil, or |
| ¼ teaspoon pepper | thyme, savory or mar- |
| 1 teaspoon garlic salt | joram |

Mix together the lamb, rice, onion, salt, pepper and garlic salt with a spoon (or with your hands) until well combined. Form into 1-inch balls. Rub the bottom of a skillet lightly with fat. Add the balls and fry until browned. (Shake the skillet to turn the balls.) Pour off the fat. Add consommé, catchup, and sweet basil or other seasoning and cover and cook *slowly* 1 hour. (When the balls are done, the rice kernels stand out to resemble porcupine needles.)

## LAMB SHOULDER CHOPS WITH MUSHROOM GARLIC SAUCE

### (2 servings)

| | |
|---|---|
| 1 clove garlic, finely chopped | Salt, pepper and paprika |
| 2 tablespoons butter | 1 can (10½ ounces) con- |
| 2 lamb shoulder chops (about | densed cream of mush- |
| ¾ inch thick) | room soup |

Fry the garlic in the butter in a skillet for a minute. Add the chops and brown on both sides in the garlic-flavored butter. Sprinkle chops with salt, pepper and paprika. Add the soup. Cover and cook slowly until the chops are fork-tender, about 45 minutes, adding a little water if the sauce seems too thick.

## LAMB CHOPS WITH BAKED BEANS

(2 servings)

2 shoulder lamb chops          ¼ cup catchup
  (about ¾ inch thick)         ½ teaspoon Worcestershire
Salt and pepper                  sauce
1½ cups (14-ounce can)         1 medium-sized sliced
  baked beans                    onion, if desired

Brown the chops on both sides in a skillet, using moderate
heat. Season with salt and pepper. Remove chops from skillet and pour in the beans, catchup and Worcestershire sauce.
Mix together. Place the onions and browned chops over the
surface. Cover and cook slowly until chops are fork-tender,
30 to 40 minutes. This can be prepared in a skillet or baked
in a shallow casserole.

## BRAISED LAMB SHOULDER CHOPS WITH PRUNES

(2 servings)

2 lamb shoulder chops          ¼ cup water and
  (about ¾ inch thick)         ¼ cup dry wine, red or white
1 tablespoon butter,           4 whole cloves
  shortening or oil              1-inch-length stick
Salt and pepper                  cinnamon
1 medium onion, sliced         2 teaspoons cornstarch
6 large dried prunes           ¼ cup cold water
½ cup water or

Brown the chops on both sides in butter in heavy frying
pan, Dutch oven, or electric skillet. Sprinkle with salt and
pepper. Place onion slices on chops. Add whole cloves, cinnamon stick, prunes, ½ cup water, or ¼ cup water and ¼ cup

Remove lamb to a pan and pour off almost all the fat. Add onion to remaining fat in the skillet and brown slightly. Add kidney beans, tomato soup, chili powder. Mix well. Place lamb pieces over surface. Cover and cook slowly until meat is fork-tender, about 45 minutes. Or, bake in a 350° F. (moderate) oven 1 hour.

*Note*: You may omit chili powder and substitute ½ teaspoon sweet basil or oregano. A different dish entirely. Serve with tortillas.

## BRAISED LAMB SHANKS WITH VEGETABLES

(4 servings)

| | |
|---|---|
| 4 lamb shanks | 1 cup carrots, diced |
| 2 tablespoons fat | 1 pound string beans, sliced |
| Salt and pepper to taste | Boiled potatoes |
| 2 cups water | Parsley |
| 1 bay leaf | 1 teaspoon Angostura bitters |
| 1 medium onion, chopped | |

Brown lamb shanks on all sides in hot fat. Sprinkle liberally with salt and pepper. Add water, bay leaf and vegetables. Cover tightly and cook over low heat on range surface, or bake in a 350° F. oven for 2 hours or until fork-tender. Remove shanks and make the gravy by allowing liquid to thicken. Add Angostura bitters. Combine shanks with gravy and simmer for a few minutes.

## SWEET AND SOUR LAMB RIBLETS WITH AN ORIENTAL SAUCE

(4 servings)

2 pounds lamb riblets, cut in halves
4 cups boiling water
1 teaspoon salt
1 tablespoon peanut or vegetable oil
¼ cup diced onion

1 cup thinly sliced carrots
1 cup pineapple tidbits or chunks
1 green pepper, cut in 1-inch squares
6 small sweet pickles, sliced

*Sauce:*

1 clove garlic, mashed with
½ teaspoon salt
1 teaspoon monosodium glutamate
2 tablespoons cornstarch
2 tablespoons brown sugar
2 tablespoons soy sauce

¼ cup vinegar
½ cup cold water
1 cup pineapple juice
1 bouillon cube (chicken or beef) dissolved in ¼ cup boiling water

Have your meat dealer chop riblets in halves. Add salt and lamb to boiling water in kettle. Cover kettle. Simmer 1 hour or until tender. Drain, saving liquid for soup or sauces. Brown the lamb pieces slowly in the oil. Mix together all of the sauce ingredients. Add to the browned lamb, and cook, stirring constantly, until sauce is transparent. Add vegetables and pineapple. Simmer mixture, covered, until vegetables are tender, but still a little crisp. Serve with steamed rice and/or fried noodles.

## SHOULDER LAMB CHOPS WITH VEGETABLES

(4 servings)

2 tablespoons butter or
   margarine
4 shoulder lamb chops, about
   1 inch thick
4 medium-sized carrots,
   sliced

½ pound mushrooms, sliced
1 medium-sized green
   pepper, sliced
½ teaspoon salt
Dash pepper
½ cup water

Melt butter or margarine. Add chops; cook until browned
on both sides. Add vegetables, seasonings and water. Cover;
cook over low heat 45 minutes, or until lamb is tender.

## LAMB TOMATO SKILLET

(6 servings)

2 eggs, beaten
¼ cup water
1½ pounds boned lamb
   shoulder, cubed
1 cup fine dry bread crumbs
¼ cup salad oil

1 10½-ounce can con-
   densed tomato soup
½ cup water
1 teaspoon dry mustard
1 teaspoon salt

Combine eggs and ¼ cup water; blend. Coat lamb with
crumbs; dip in egg mixture. Coat with crumbs again. Heat
oil. Add lamb and cook until lightly browned on all sides.
Combine remaining ingredients and blend. Pour over lamb.
Cover and cook over low heat 30 to 40 minutes, or until
lamb is tender.

## SWEDISH LAMB MEAT BALLS

(4 to 6 servings)

1 pound ground lamb
½ cup fine dry bread crumbs
1 egg, slightly beaten
2 cups sour cream
1 teaspoon salt

⅛ teaspoon pepper
¼ teaspoon nutmeg
¼ teaspoon allspice
¼ cup butter or margarine

Combine lamb, crumbs, egg, ¼ cup cream and seasonings; blend. Shape into 1-inch balls. Melt butter or margarine. Add lamb meat balls and cook until lightly browned on all sides. Cover and cook 15 minutes. Gradually add remaining cream and heat to serving temperature.

## LAMB SPAGHETTI DINNER

(6 servings)

2 pounds boneless lamb
    shoulder, diced
Melted butter or
    margarine
1 medium-sized onion,
    chopped

3 6-ounce cans tomato paste
2½ cups water
1½ teaspoons oregano
    Salt and pepper to taste
1 pound spaghetti

Cook lamb in small amount of butter or margarine until browned on all sides. Add onion, tomato paste and 2½ cups water; heat to boiling point, stirring occasionally. Cook, covered, over low heat, 45 minutes. Add oregano and salt and pepper; mix well. Meanwhile, cook spaghetti in boiling salted water. Drain in colander. Serve lamb sauce over spaghetti.

## LAMB AND PEPPERS

(4 to 6 servings)

2 tablespoons butter or margarine

1½ pounds boneless lamb shoulder, diced

3 medium-sized green peppers, diced

1 small onion, coarsely chopped

2 canned pimientos, diced

Salt and pepper to taste

Melt butter or margarine; add lamb and cook until lightly browned on all sides. Add green peppers, onion and pimientos; cover and cook over low heat 45 minutes, or until lamb is tender. Season with salt and pepper.

## SAUTÉED LAMB SHOULDER AND MUSHROOMS

(4 servings)

2 tablespoons butter or margarine

1 4-ounce can mushroom stems and pieces, drained

1 pound boned lamb shoulder, sliced about ⅛ inch thick

Salt and pepper to taste

4 slices buttered toast

Melt butter or margarine; add mushrooms and cook over low heat until lightly browned. Add lamb and cook until lightly browned on both sides. Season with salt and pepper. Arrange lamb and mushrooms on toast.

## LAMB SKILLET DINNER

(4 to 6 servings)

2 tablespoons butter or
   margarine
1 medium-sized onion,
   chopped
1 cup sliced celery
1½ pounds boned lamb
   shoulder, diced
1 cup water

1 tablespoon all-purpose
   flour
Salt and pepper to taste
2 medium-sized tomatoes,
   sliced
Salt and pepper
3 cups seasoned mashed
   potatoes

Melt butter or margarine; add onion and celery and sauté until tender. Add lamb and cook over low heat until browned on all sides. Add water; cover and cook 45 minutes, or until lamb is tender. Add a little of hot mixture to flour; blend. Add to remaining hot mixture and cook over low heat, stirring constantly, until thickened. Season with salt and pepper. Top lamb mixture with tomatoes; sprinkle with salt and pepper and top with potatoes. Broil 3 to 4 inches from source of heat 5 minutes, or until potatoes are lightly browned.

## BREADED LAMB CHOPS WITH GRAVY

(4 servings)

1½ cups milk
¾ teaspoon salt
⅛ teaspoon pepper
4 shoulder lamb chops,
   about ¾ inch thick
1 egg, beaten

2 tablespoons water
½ cup fine dry bread
   crumbs
¼ cup butter or margarine
2 tablespoons all-purpose
   flour

Combine milk, salt and pepper. Add chops. Cover and cook over low heat 1 hour. Drain; reserve liquid. Combine egg and water. Coat chops with crumbs; dip in egg. Coat with crumbs again. Melt butter or margarine. Add chops and cook until lightly browned on both sides. Remove chops. Combine flour with milk mixture; blend. Add to drippings and cook over low heat, stirring constantly until thickened.

## CHINESE LAMB SKILLET

(6 servings)

| | |
|---|---|
| 2 tablespoons salad oil | ¼ cup honey |
| 2½ pounds lamb shoulder, boned and cubed | 1 teaspoon salt |
| | ¼ teaspoon pepper |
| 2 1-pound cans Chinese vegetables | 1 tablespoon soy sauce |
| | 2 tablespoons cornstarch |
| ½ cup vinegar | Cooked rice |

Heat oil. Add lamb and cook until lightly browned on all sides. Drain off drippings. Add Chinese vegetables, vinegar, honey, salt, pepper and soy sauce to lamb. Cover and cook over low heat 2 hours, stirring occasionally. Remove lamb. Add a little of hot mixture to cornstarch; blend. Add to remaining hot mixture. Cook over low heat, stirring constantly, until thickened and clear. Add lamb. Serve over rice.

## LAMB-RICE PILAF

(6 servings)

| | |
|---|---|
| 3 tablespoons butter or margarine | 2 tablespoons salad oil |
| 1 medium-sized onion, chopped | 1½ pounds boneless lamb shoulder, cubed |
| 1½ cups uncooked rice | 2 medium-sized tomatoes, sliced |
| 3 cups beef stock or bouillon | 2 teaspoons salt |
| | ¼ teaspoon pepper |

Melt butter or margarine; add onion and rice and cook over low heat until rice is lightly browned. Add beef stock or bouillon; heat to boiling point. Cover and cook over low heat 15 minutes. Meanwhile, heat oil in a heavy skillet; add lamb and cook until lightly browned on all sides. Add lamb mixture and remaining ingredients to rice mixture. Cook, covered, 20 minutes, or until lamb is tender.

## LAMB PILAF

(6 servings)

1½ to 2 pounds boneless
    lamb, cut in 1-inch
    cubes
1 tablespoon fat
1 medium onion, diced
2 tablespoons butter
1½ cups uncooked rice
1½ teaspoons salt
¼ teaspoon pepper

¼ teaspoon basil
½ teaspoon oregano
1 8-ounce can tomato sauce
2 cups bouillon (made by
    dissolving 2 bouillon
    cubes in 2 cups boil-
    ing water) or
Stock from lamb bones

Melt fat in a skillet. Brown lamb cubes on all sides in melted fat, using moderate heat. Remove meat from skillet. Cook the onion slowly in the melted butter until onions are golden-translucent in color. Add the uncooked rice and seasonings to this mixture; cook until rice is lightly browned. Place half of the browned lamb in the bottom of a 2-quart casserole, then a layer of the rice mixture, then more lamb, with the remainder of the rice on top. Combine the tomato sauce and the bouillon or stock. Pour about ½ of the liquid over the lamb-rice. Cover and bake at 350° F., adding more liquid as needed. Bake about 1 hour or until all liquid is absorbed, and the lamb is fork-tender.

walnuts, or almonds; crumbled crisp bacon; finely chopped hard-cooked egg; shredded coconut; raisins; chopped preserved ginger; minced parsley; thinly sliced green onions—tops and all; chopped sweet pickle; shredded pineapple; shrimps, fish.

## FRIKADELLER—SWEDISH MEAT CAKES

### (14 meat cakes, 2½ inches in diameter)

| | |
|---|---|
| 1 pound lean ground lamb | ½ teaspoon salt |
| 2 eggs, unbeaten | Dash of pepper |
| 6 tablespoons undiluted evaporated milk | ¼ teaspoon thyme, if desired |
| 1 tablespoon flour | 1 tablespoon minced or grated onion |

Using a fork, whip all together until really fluffy. Mixture will be quite soft. Refrigerate until ready to use. Place slightly rounded tablespoonfuls of the lamb mixture in melted butter on moderately hot griddle, smoothing each patty out until about 2½ inches in diameter. When nicely browned on one side, about 3 minutes, turn and brown other side about 3 minutes. Do not cook fast.

## CREAMED LAMB SHORT RIBS

### (4 to 6 servings)

| | |
|---|---|
| 2 pounds lamb short ribs | 1 teaspoon salt |
| ⅓ cup water | ¼ teaspoon pepper |
| 2 tablespoons all-purpose flour | ¼ cup chopped parsley |
| | 1 cup milk |
| 2 tablespoons grated onion | 1 teaspoon Angostura bitters |

Cook short ribs over low heat until browned on all sides. Add water. Cover and cook 30 minutes. Drain off drippings. Add flour, onion, salt, pepper and parsley to lamb, and blend. Gradually add milk and Angostura bitters and cook over low heat, stirring constantly, until thickened. Serve garnished with additional parsley, as desired.

## LAMB RIBLET AND RICE SKILLET

**(4 servings)**

| | |
|---|---|
| 2 pounds lamb riblets | ½ cup uncooked rice |
| 2 cups water | Salt and pepper to taste |
| 1 1½-ounce package dehydrated onion soup mix | |

Cook riblets until browned on all sides. Add water and soup mix. Heat to boiling point. Add rice and salt and pepper; mix well. Cover and cook over low heat, stirring occasionally, until rice and lamb are tender, about 25 to 30 minutes.

## LAMB NECK SLICES WITH MINT SAUCE

**(6 servings)**

| | |
|---|---|
| 2 tablespoons butter or margarine | 1 teaspoon rosemary |
| | Salt and pepper to taste |
| 6 lamb neck slices, about ¾ inch thick | 1 cup lamb stock or chicken bouillon |
| ½ cup chopped celery | ½ cup chopped mint |
| 2 tablespoons all-purpose flour | |

## DEVILED LAMB SPARERIBS

(4 servings)

2½-3 pounds lamb spareribs,
   cut in serving pieces
2 tablespoons prepared
   mustard
1 cup all-purpose flour
2 teaspoons salt
¼ teaspoon pepper
⅓ cup shortening

½ cup chili sauce
½ cup lemon juice
2 tablespoons
   Worcestershire sauce
½ teaspoon paprika
¼ cup chopped onion
2 cups water

Brush lamb with mustard. Sprinkle with flour, salt and pepper. Melt shortening; add lamb. Cook until browned on both sides. Combine remaining ingredients and pour over lamb. Cover and simmer 1½ hours or until lamb is tender.

## BRAISED LAMB RIBLETS

(4 servings)

2 pounds lamb riblets
1 tablespoon melted butter
   or margarine
½ cup sliced celery
2 large onions, sliced
2 cups vegetable juice
   cocktail

2 tablespoons all-purpose
   flour
1 tablespoon vinegar
Salt and onion salt to taste

Cook lamb in butter or margarine until well browned on all sides. Drain off drippings. Add celery, onions and 1¾ cups vegetable juice cocktail; cover and cook over low heat 1 hour, or until lamb is tender. Combine flour and remaining vegetable juice cocktail; blend. Gradually add flour mixture to lamb; cook over low heat, stirring constantly, until thickened. Add remaining ingredients; mix well.

## LAMB CABBAGE ROLLS

(8 servings)

8 cabbage leaves
1 pound ground lamb
1 cup finely chopped
  potatoes
2 tablespoons chopped onion
  Dash thyme

Dash pepper
1 teaspoon salt
1 10½-ounce can
  condensed tomato soup
⅔ cup water

Cook cabbage leaves in boiling salted water about 3 minutes; drain. Combine lamb, potatoes, onion, thyme, pepper and salt; mix well. Place 2 or 3 tablespoons of mixture on each cabbage leaf. Fold leaf. Place in large saucepan. Add soup and water. Cover; cook over low heat about 40 minutes, or until cabbage is tender.

## LAMB SUPPER ROLLS

(4 to 6 servings)

½ cup butter or margarine
½ pound mushrooms, sliced
1 cup soft bread crumbs
1 teaspoon Worcestershire
  sauce

1 teaspoon salt
⅛ teaspoon pepper
1½ pounds boneless lamb
  shoulder, thinly sliced

Melt ¼ cup butter or margarine; add mushrooms and cook until lightly browned. Add crumbs, Worcestershire sauce, salt and pepper; mix well. Spread on lamb slices. Roll up

# GARNISHES AND RELISHES

*Lamb is wonderful all by itself—but just for a change try some of these garnishes and relishes for extra appetite appeal.*

■▪▪■▪▪■▪▪■▪▪■▪▪■▪▪■▪▪■▪▪■▪▪■▪▪■▪▪■▪▪■▪▪■▪▪■▪▪■▪▪■▪▪■▪▪■▪

Top canned pear halves, peach halves, orange slices with mint jelly.

Canned pineapple rings with mint jelly or a spiced crab apple in the center.

Cinnamon apple rings. (Raw apple rings cooked in red cinnamon sirup to cover.) To make this cinnamon sirup add red cinnamon candies to water and simmer. Add enough candies to produce a light red color.

**MINT MERINGUE PEARS** Beat 2 egg whites until stiff. Add ½ cup mint jelly and continue beating until well mixed. Put mint meringue on cut surface of each pear half (fresh or canned), and place in oven or broiler just long enough to become lightly browned. Serve hot.

Orange shells filled with cranberry sauce.

Minted pears, pineapple or apples made by simmering fruit in mint-flavored sirup with green coloring added. (Fresh or canned fruits may be used.)

Fresh or canned pear halves with currant jelly or plum jelly.

Spiced whole peaches or apricots. Your grocer has them.

Guava jelly on orange slices.

Chili sauce or piccalilli in tiny paper cups.

Molded individual fruit or vegetable salads in lettuce cups.

Fresh or canned peach halves filled with chutney.

**CLARET SPICED PRUNES** Soak overnight 24 large prunes in 1 cup claret wine and 1 cup water. Next morning, add a 3-inch stick of cinnamon and 12 whole cloves. Simmer ½ hour. Stir in ⅓ cup sugar during last few minutes of cooking. Chill before serving.


## MINTED ONION SLICES

| | |
|---|---|
| 3 large sweet Spanish onions | Salt |
| 6 tender mint leaves, chopped | Coarse-ground black pepper |
| 1 tablespoon minced parsley | ½ cup olive or salad oil |
| 1 teaspoon minced fresh thyme *or* | ¼ cup red wine vinegar |
| ¼ teaspoon crushed dry thyme | |

Chill onions. Slice them crosswise about ¼ inch thick. Mix together the mint, parsley and thyme. In a flat dish arrange

## CRANBERRY CHUTNEY I

(Makes 1 pint)

1 1-pound can whole          ½ cup finely chopped celery
    cranberry sauce          1 teaspoon powdered ginger
½ cup raisins
½ unpeeled, cored apple,
    chopped

Combine all ingredients. Store in refrigerator for several hours so that flavors may be thoroughly blended.

## CRANBERRY CHUTNEY II

(Makes 1 pint)

1 can (1 pound) whole          ¼ cup finely chopped
    cranberry sauce              almonds
2 tablespoons light brown      ¼ teaspoon garlic salt
    sugar          ¼ teaspoon ground ginger
1 tablespoon vinegar          ⅛ teaspoon red pepper
¼ cup seedless raisins

Combine ingredients. Chill thoroughly for flavors to blend.

## CRANBERRY ALMOND RELISH

(Makes 2 cups)

1 1-pound can whole          3 tablespoons lemon juice
    cranberry sauce          ⅔ cup blanched almonds,
2 tablespoons orange              halved or chopped
    marmalade              walnuts or pecans

Combine whole cranberry sauce, orange marmalade, and lemon juice. Blanch almonds and remove skins (better yet, use canned blanched almonds). Cut in halves. Cool. Stir into cranberry marmalade mixture. Serve well chilled.

## SPICY CRANBERRY RELISH

(Makes 2 cups)

1 1-pound can whole cranberry sauce (or jellied, crushed)
½ cup drained crushed pineapple (8- or 9-ounce can)

¼ teaspoon cinnamon
¼ teaspoon mace or nutmeg
¼ teaspoon powdered mustard

Mix thoroughly. Place in refrigerator an hour or more for flavors to blend.

## CRANBERRY GINGER PEACHES

(8 servings)

1 1-pound can whole cranberry sauce, drained
½ cup raisins
½ lemon (with rind), ground

1 teaspoon ginger
8 canned peach halves, drained

Combine cranberry sauce, raisins, ground lemon and ginger. Chill thoroughly. Place a heaping tablespoon of relish in the center of each peach half.

## CRANBERRY APPLE RELISH

(Makes 2 cups)

1 unpeeled apple (medium tart)
½ cup diced celery
¼ teaspoon salt

2 tablespoons bottled horse-radish
1 1-pound can whole cranberry sauce

Toast bread on one side. Combine remaining ingredients; blend. Spread on untoasted sides of bread. Broil 3 to 4 inches from source of heat 8 to 10 minutes, or until lightly browned.

## GOURMET LAMBURGERS

(6 servings)

1½  pounds ground lamb
¼  cup chopped onion
¼  cup dry red wine
1  egg, beaten
1  teaspoon salt

⅛  teaspoon pepper
½  teaspoon lamb herbs
    (rosemary, dry mint
    leaves and grated
    orange rind)

Combine all ingredients; mix well. Shape into 6 patties. Broil 3 to 4 inches from source of heat 5 to 6 minutes, or until browned on both sides.

## BARBECUED CHEESE LAMBURGERS

(4 sandwiches)

2  tablespoons butter or margarine
1  medium-sized onion, chopped
¾  cup chili sauce
½  cup vinegar
2  teaspoons Worcestershire sauce
   Salt and pepper to taste

1  pound ground lamb shoulder
½  teaspoon dry mustard
1  teaspoon salt
¼  teaspoon pepper
2  slices processed Swiss cheese, cut in thin strips
4  hamburger rolls, split and toasted

Melt butter or margarine; add onion and cook until lightly browned. Add chili sauce, vinegar, Worcestershire sauce and salt and pepper to taste; mix well. Cook over low heat 20 minutes. Combine lamb, mustard, salt and pepper; mix well. Shape into 4 1-inch patties and place on broiler rack. Broil 3 to 4 inches from source of heat 5 minutes. Turn; broil 4 minutes or to desired degree of doneness. Top with cheese; broil 2 minutes. Serve on rolls with chili sauce mixture.

## LAMBURGERS WITH MUSTARD SAUCE

(4 sandwiches)

| | |
|---|---|
| 2 egg yolks, well beaten | 1 tablespoon chopped |
| ¼ cup vinegar | parsley |
| 2 teaspoons dry mustard | ¼ teaspoon marjoram |
| 2 teaspoons salt | 2 tablespoons finely chopped |
| ½ cup mayonnaise | onion |
| Dash Tabasco sauce | 4 hamburger rolls, split and |
| 1 pound ground lamb | toasted |
| shoulder | |

Combine egg yolks, vinegar, mustard and 1 teaspoon salt. Cook over low heat, stirring constantly, until thickened. Add mayonnaise and Tabasco sauce; blend. Combine lamb, parsley, marjoram, onion and remaining 1 teaspoon salt; mix well. Shape into 4 1-inch patties. Broil 3 to 4 inches from source of heat 5 minutes; turn. Broil 5 minutes, or to desired degree of doneness. Serve on rolls with mustard sauce.

## LAMB CHILIBURGERS

(4 servings)

2 tablespoons butter or
  margarine
1 pound ground lamb
  shoulder
1 medium-sized onion,
  chopped
1 1-pound can kidney beans

2 cups tomato juice
2 tablespoons all-purpose
  flour
¼ teaspoon chili powder
  Salt and pepper to taste
4 hamburger rolls, split and
  toasted

Melt butter or margarine; add lamb and onion and cook over low heat, stirring occasionally, until lightly browned. Add beans and tomato juice; heat to boiling point. Cook over low heat 30 minutes. Add a small amount of hot mixture to flour; blend. Add to remaining hot mixture and cook over low heat, stirring constantly, until thickened. Add chili powder and salt and pepper; mix well. Serve over hamburger rolls.

## STUFFED LAMBURGERS

(4 servings)

Make 8 patties to a pound of ground lamb, flattening each cake to a ⅛-inch thickness. Place a slice of natural or process Cheddar cheese, a spoonful of minced onion, or a dollop of butter creamed with herbs—fresh or dry—on one of the thin patties. Top with a second patty and press the edges together tightly so the filling won't come out during the cooking process. Broil or fry. Don't overcook. Have the lamb patty a crusty brown outside with a slight pink tinge to the interior. Turn once. Season with salt and pepper after turning. Add a dash of thyme, a sprinkling of garlic salt or

curry powder, or depend upon the mustard, catchup, barbecue sauce, relish or what-have-you to add that little fillip
of flavor. Serve between two sandwich bun halves, buttered
before browning on the griddle.

# Lamburger Sandwich Variations

These provide plenty of opportunity for individual styling
in lamburger architecture. You'll find ideas here:

**1. Cheese:**  Place slice of Cheddar cheese under or over
the hot lamburger—in the bun. Serve with small whole
tomatoes, to be eaten out of hand.

**2. Blue Cheese:**  Combine ¼ pound Blue cheese, crumbled,
with 2 tablespoons softened butter, and ½ to 1 teaspoon
Worcestershire sauce. Cream well. Top each lamburger,
immediately after turning, with a teaspoon of the mixture.
Serve between slices of hot French bread, adrip with butter.
Celery goes well with these.

**3. Beans:**  Heat a can of baked beans or chili beans. Place
grilled lamburger on lower toasted bun half. Top with a
spoonful of the beans. Add the bun "lid." Serve with dill
pickles or green onions.

**4. Tower of Pisa:**  Place cooked lamburger on toasted bun
half. Add mayonnaise, India relish, slice of sweet Spanish
onion, tomato slice, lettuce, slice of dill pickle. Top with
mayonnaise-spread bun half. Wrap with a paper napkin and
—hang on!

**5. Double Decker:**  Make *thin* lamb patties—8 to a pound
of ground lamb, allowing two for a bun. Grill quickly. Place

# INDEX

# How to Roast

1. Season with salt and pepper, if desired.
2. Place fat side up on rack in open roasting pan.
3. Insert meat thermometer.
4. Roast in slow oven—300° F.
5. Add no water. Do not cover. Do not baste.
6. Roast to desired degree of doneness.

# How to Broil

1. Set the oven regulator for broiling.
2. Place meat 2 to 3 inches from heat.
3. Broil until the top of meat is brown.
4. Season with salt and pepper.
5. Turn the meat and brown the other side.
6. Season and serve at once.

# How to Panbroil

1. Place meat in heavy frying-pan. Cook slowly.
2. Do not add fat or water. Do not cover.
3. Turn occasionally to insure even cooking.
4. Pour fat from pan as it accumulates.
5. Brown meat on both sides.
6. Do not overcook. Season.

# How to Panfry

1. Season meat and dredge with flour or corn meal, if desired.
2. Brown quickly on each side in a small amount of fat.
3. Do not cover.
4. Cook at moderate temperature until done, turning occasionally.
5. Drain and serve at once.